LIFE
UNLIMITED

Dear Cindy,

    I'm so deeply grateful that you're a part of my life. Thank you for shining your light so brightly. You bring me joy.

    With love and profound respect,

LIFE
UNLIMITED

A Timeless Approach to
Aging and Longevity

Edward Franco

iUniverse, Inc.
Bloomington

Life Unlimited
A Timeless Approach to Aging and Longevity

iUniverse books may be ordered through booksellers or by contacting:

iUniverse
1663 Liberty Drive
Bloomington, IN 47403
www.iuniverse.com
1-800-Authors (1-800-288-4677)

Because of the dynamic nature of the Internet, any web addresses or
links contained in this book may have changed since publication and
may no longer be valid. The views expressed in this work are solely those
of the author and do not necessarily reflect the views of the publisher,
and the publisher hereby disclaims any responsibility for them.

The information presented in this book is intended to help
improve your overall sense of well-being. It is not a substitute
for appropriate medical care or mental health counseling.

ISBN: 978-1-4502-6017-6 (sc)
ISBN: 978-1-4502-6019-0 (hc)
ISBN: 978-1-4502-6018-3 (e)

Printed in the United States of America

iUniverse rev. date: 11/11/2011

For Jim, Gene, and Franco—
without whom it would make little sense to live forever.

Contents

Preface

My intention for this book is that, in some small but meaningful way, it will enhance and facilitate your personal process of discovery. The very act of your picking it up tells me it is likely you sense something shifting inside you, something that says no to conventional thinking about aging and yes to the myriad possibilities of life in the third millennium. Those of us who are alive today have been given an incredible gift, the opportunity to make a momentous choice: We must either evolve or perish. This book, which would not have been published a mere twenty years ago, is about choosing the former.

When I was a kid, some part of me believed in magic. I still do. This is not a part of me that I want to "grow up" so I can act my age. I love the fact that I still have the zeal and wonder of a child. And, in essence, that is what I'll be asking of you—to let yourself believe, as a child might, that you can create your own personal heaven. As we explore this new frontier together, we will be looking at the collective attitudes and beliefs that we hold on the subjects of aging and death. It is my contention that we have lost our way in a world that could so readily be paradise. If there exists a heaven anywhere, there can exist a heaven here.

When I initially sat down with the idea of writing a book on physical immortality, the first thought I had was, "It's too outrageous—who would read it?" Of course, by its very definition, the New Age encompasses thoughts and beliefs yet unexplored. Thankfully, there have been courageous voices that have broached this subject, either directly or indirectly, before me. And so, to Sondra Ray and Dr. Deepak Chopra, for their insight, truth, and courage, I extend my heartfelt thanks. May they live forever in peace.

This book is far wiser than I am. Although I fervently nurtured and cultivated its contents, I was more curator than author of the ideas found in its pages. The process took much longer than I had anticipated. On more than one occasion I tried to convince myself that I held a completed manuscript in my hands. It eventually became clear that it was a living entity of sorts, one whose birth could not be artificially induced. It gives me immense joy to think that the book now rests contentedly in the hands of you, the reader.

Acknowledgments

For their contribution, inspiration, love, encouragement, kindness, and/or sense of humor, the author extends his sincere gratitude to the following:

Ron Edens
James Fox
Sumiko Fox
Katie Franco
Louise Franco
Paul Franco
Louise Gent-Sandford
Marilyn McCarthy
Jennie Parker
Theodora Parker
Boris Pisman
Pups
Sondra Ray
Franco Scala
Glasco Amgott Stern
Michael Wawrzynski

Chapter 1

New Game, New Rules

To PONDER THE IDEA of unlimited life—of living a joyous, disease-free existence, one in which even death has been conquered—is to test the very fabric of our being, our soul, our sanity. Until recently, such thoughts would have been universally condemned as folly or madness and, to this day, are still regarded as such by just about everyone.

And yet, one of the very exciting aspects of life on this planet at this time is the degree to which there are open minds willing to embrace new paradigms. All around the globe, people are realizing that we have more influence over our personal destinies than we had ever dreamed possible. We are powerful beings, no denying that. But equally true is the fact that many of us have covered up or hidden our power for fear of shining too brightly, or worse, actively misused or misdirected it and created suffering for ourselves through our very belief in its necessity. As our consciousness as humans expands, it makes sense that we would increasingly explore the heart of our convictions. What do we truly believe about God, about life, and about death? Maybe the New Age should more aptly be called the New Aging, as it is so swiftly redefining how we view the process of growing older. The old paradigm lies prostrate in awe of and in service to sickness, aging, and death. Ironically, that model itself is now aged and dying.

We stand at the threshold of discovery. We live in a time far more rich and exciting than any other in history. Everything that has been taken for granted for aeons, from the origin of the universe up to and including the inevitability of death, is now being questioned. In return, it seems we are being asked to adopt change and alter our notions in ways that have not been asked of us previously. Although in some cases as daunting and challenging as they are novel, these demands are not without their rewards. Over the last hundred years, we have seen mind-boggling advances in science, medicine, and technology. Consider how outlandish the idea of in vitro fertilization, cloning, or stem cell therapy would have been a century ago. Indeed, that which is accepted as science today was not even in the realm of science fiction a hundred years ago. On the sociocultural and humanistic fronts, the whole self-help movement (spawning books by Louise Hay, Wayne Dyer, and the like) was an unforeseen entity. There has no doubt been a change in consciousness. People want to know, more than ever before, what their lives and life itself are about. No longer silent pioneers, we are speaking up and talking back.

We have also witnessed a major breakthrough in the attitudes of the general public and the medical profession toward holistic modalities. Can you imagine a Harvard-educated physician a mere generation ago writing books such as those Andrew Weil now pens? Probably not. Clearly life is going through its own metamorphosis, with most of us rarely stopping to consider just how rapidly things are changing. But changing they are.

During this present period of evolution, some spiritualists are saying that time itself is speeding up—that is, things are manifesting more quickly. Put plainly, there is no time left for sitting on the fence. And there's no better time than now to play an active role in manifesting the true beauty of life, much of which currently exists only as potential. It requires only our commitment to doing so.

A key underlying principle running throughout this book is that our thoughts are a potent source of creation and manifestation. Although they cannot be seen or heard outside our heads, our thoughts have as much power and pull as anything physical we might create. The mind/body connection, as it is commonly called, has reached a level of acceptance to the point where even many traditional doctors will concede that positive, life-affirming thoughts in the face of physical illness can do no harm and could possibly even do some good. Put in the simplest way, the essential tenet behind mind/body medicine is that our thoughts have a real and actual impact on our bodies. For the physicians who spearheaded mind/body medicine, this has long been a well-established fact used to patients' advantages (see *Quantum Healing* by Deepak Chopra or *Love, Medicine & Miracles* by Bernie Siegel on the suggested reading list).

Your experience of reading this book will be greatly enhanced if you keep your personal vision of life in the years ahead close at hand. What do *you* see? Is it a world without sickness, without famine, without war? It is all possible. As our conscious awareness grows, we cannot help but manifest unprecedented change. And that change begins with the recognition of the power of our thoughts.

I would like to make clear from the outset that I have no special talent, gift, or connection to the divine, nor am I one of a chosen few. You do not have to do any particular thing *in form* to walk toward physical immortality. It's not so much about behavior as it is about perception and belief.

I'd also like to introduce you, right at the start, to two words that are likely not a part of your present vocabulary: "deathist" and "immortalist," representing opposite ends of a life philosophy. One whose beliefs are deathist is one who believes in the inevitability of death, with each passing day bringing them closer to the void of nonexistence or the gates of heaven, depending on their faith orientation. By way of contrast, one whose beliefs are immortalist believes that life can lead to a greater expression of itself and ultimately become ongoing in any way one desires—in spirit, if they choose to leave the physical body, or in form, if they choose to remain incarnate.

Let's acknowledge that we live, by and large, in a deathist society. Walk into any greeting card store, and you will find a variety of cards subliminally proclaiming the inevitability of death through their ostensibly humorous portrayal of birthdays as dreaded, horrible things. Certainly no one would deny that our "number" increases with the passing years. But what says that this number must also dictate how we look, feel, or act? Nothing. No thing. We alone decide the effect time will have on us. But I'm getting ahead of myself.

As a people, we operate on a mostly unconscious level where the issue of death is concerned. We tend to avoid discussing it at all costs. Perhaps upon accumulating a certain amount of wealth or reaching an age we perceive as a milestone, we may, in the spirit of being dutiful citizens, go about the business of preparing a will. And some of us, particularly those with families, might purchase life insurance as a means of protecting our loved ones in the event of our untimely demise. With the exception of these two fleeting examples, death is not something we are usually willing to look at. But such denial comes at a very substantial price.

Several prominent persons on the forefront of the immortalist movement, most notably Sondra Ray, the mother of the rebirthing community, have theorized that the single most significant cause of aging and death is the unconscious thought that death is *inevitable*. From a very young age, we are indoctrinated with this idea. Even a commonplace bedtime prayer for children, *Now I Lay Me Down to Sleep*, includes the line, "Should I die before I wake, I pray the Lord my soul to take." If our thoughts directly affect our wellness, what is the sweeping consequence of the fact that virtually all of us walk around holding the thought, "Death is inevitable," as one of our core beliefs? Perhaps the biggest leap of faith I will ask you to make while reading this book is the idea that this thought may be killing us, if for no other reason than because it is so widely and uniformly accepted as an inviolate fact, and so very few individuals have questioned its hold on us for fear of appearing foolish, stupid, or just plain nuts. If we allow for a moment that aging or death could be hastened as a result of this unconscious thought, then keeping it hidden in darkness won't serve us. What it does is fuel the aging process as an unconscious act.

Think, now, of the typical image of an average 90-year-old man or woman. It's likely you'll envision someone with physical limitations, wrinkled skin, low energy, and poor flexibility. But if I asked you to visualize that same person at eighteen years of age, you probably wouldn't see any of that. I would like to propose that all or most of those dramatic signs of aging could be prevented if two things were different: (1) if the belief that death is inevitable were removed from the collective unconscious, and (2) if we remained consciously aware of the external factors that influence our aging process. You don't just wake up one morning and find yourself old and bent over. It happens slowly, over time. But it happens that way for a reason. And that reason is the lack of conscious awareness around matters related to aging. If we greet each morning thinking, "I am a greater expression of myself today than I have ever been before," the transition into an aged being need not occur. This brings us to a central point in immortalist ideology.

We need to heal our relationship with death before we can heal our relationship with life. If, after careful soul-searching, we reach the conclusion that death is inevitable, then our assignment is to make peace with that fact and to follow our inner guidance as to the steps involved in doing so. A decision made consciously would yield a related life philosophy as a natural consequence. Similarly, if we come to the decision that we can live as long as we choose, that would dictate a mode of living congruent with that belief. It probably goes without saying that the latter choice is the more difficult road, at least at this time, as there is still very little social support for this way of thinking. The bottom line is that we need to be at peace with the decision we make. Either decision made consciously and with intention will serve us better than one made by default.

The old worldview of an anthropomorphic God (i.e., the old man with the white beard sitting in the heavens) is basically viewed through the eyes of the enlightened as a creation of the male ego. God is not male or female and does not have genitals. God is the animating force for good that moves in and through us, fueling our spiritual essence. It is an integral part of each and every one of us. The new model of eternal life posits that we can be one with God without having to die. For if God also lives within us, destroying the body is akin to destroying a living manifestation of God.

The idea of self-realization and how it relates to aging and longevity will be closely examined in subsequent chapters. As we go forward, I ask you to allow that there exists at least the *possibility* of a new world order that far exceeds our current one. Do not let the objective nature of science keep you from an idea that your heart might otherwise embrace. Science is a relative discipline that would once have told us the world is flat and the sun revolves around the earth. I like to think of it this way: The mind can blind, but the heart is smart. So let's begin an exploration of the heart, one which, it is my sincere wish, will illustrate that you have a far greater say in your own aging process than you might have previously thought possible.

We'll start by looking at the things we've been told about life and death, things you might not have consciously looked at before.

Chapter 2

Invisible Monsters

BECAUSE WE HAVE BEEN relentlessly taught that death is inevitable, and because no one has yet scientifically proven what happens after one dies, many of us live with the fear of its looming presence. This is not a fear we usually address directly, but rather one we let silently brew and fester. Instead of contemplating the significance of death as a force in our lives, we sidestep the issue altogether. It's almost as if we've been brainwashed into avoiding the idea through subservient passivity. No wonder death is sometimes called the big sleep.

But our unconscious thoughts are as impactful as our conscious ones and should not be disregarded. We may profess to be excited about the life we're living and our prospects for the future, but if we believe in the inevitability of death, then, just as certainly, a shadow hangs over that future. That is to say, if we view each new day as another day closer to the grave, how could we ever believe in the promise of what lies ahead? Conversely, if we know, feel, and believe that we are loved and cherished by a God whose will it is that we *live*, the future becomes something to welcome and celebrate.

Ask someone if they would like to live forever, and you will quickly uncover their core concept as to what life is, or must eventually become. Invariably, the responses received will be peppered with thoughts like, "There's too much pain and misery in the world," or "Life isn't fair," or "Why would I want to live forever when I don't even know why I'm here in the first place?"

For most of us, just contemplating the idea of unlimited life prompts overwhelming feelings and debilitating anxiety. Our mind starts to race with questions: What would I do with all that time? What would I feel like? What will I look like? Will I have enough money? We all know that life involves work and the idea of it continuing without end seems daunting. "Don't I deserve a rest?" we might ask. These are exactly the kinds of questions that must be contemplated—and answered—if we are to have lasting joy in our lives.

Again, if we are to heal our relationship with life, we first must heal our relationship with death. But healing is always a conscious choice. Many of us were spoon fed dogma from a very early age and have been conditioned to look outside ourselves for the causes of—or maybe more accurately, the blame for—the things we don't understand. We also do an excellent job of suppressing joy much of the time. Even loving parents willingly impart the "facts" of mortality to their children, lest they grow up delusional and unaware that they too are doomed to certain death. In our incessant urge to rationalize our mistakes, we have taken something we've created (death), designated it preordained, and—since appearances imply we are unable to do anything about it—concocted reasons why it must be God's will. But what God that loved its children would decree that they fall prey to aging, sickness, and death? Perhaps Voltaire said it best when he said, "God created man in His image, and then man returned the compliment." For just as surely as wars and famines exist and are not God's will, so it is with death.

As you begin to attune your ear to the societal message, "You have to die," you'll notice that the voices are numerous, varied, often well hidden, and sometimes well buried. Who was the first person to tell you that you wouldn't live forever? Was it a clergy member? A teacher? A parent? Realize that they were telling you what they themselves had been taught many years prior. As human consciousness evolves, what was once accurate and valid may no longer be so. We can consciously choose to reject outdated ideas. It's a choice we have to make—and will make—one way or the other. You decide if you stay alive or not, even though the voice of the world says you are powerless over that decision.

Take some time now to think about the ways in which death has played a role in your life. Ask yourself the following questions:

1. What were you taught about death while you were growing up? For example, I can recall being nine years old and being told by a friend that after we die, we go to a place called purgatory, which he described as "like hell, but only for a little while." Make a list of the things you were told about death while still a child. Include seemingly innocuous expressions like "buy the farm," "kick the bucket," "cash in your chips," et cetera.

2. What have been your personal experiences with death during your life thus far? Have you lost anyone who was close to you? If so, who were they? How did they die? What did you conclude as a result of their passing? How do you feel about them today? Did they ever share their beliefs about death with you? If so, what were they?

3. What are your thoughts about your own life expectancy? Can you picture yourself alive at seventy? At eighty? Keep upping the number until you reach an age where it seems impossible to believe that you would still be alive. Will you be alive at one hundred? What happens at a hundred and ten? How about a hundred and twenty?

4. If you are able to see yourself as alive at an "advanced" age, what do you look like? Are you in any way feeble or debilitated? Remember that the objective of physical

immortality is as much about the quality of life as it is about the number of its years.

5. If you were to survive indefinitely, what would your life be like with regard to family and friends? Are you a sole survivor? Has everyone you've loved died by the time you reach one hundred? If you cannot conceive of those you love remaining alive with you, that could greatly affect your desire to hang around.

As humans, we often fear time, thinking it will rob us of our agility, physical health, and cognitive abilities. But time can also be an ally. If we stay mindful of our thought processes, consciously choosing thoughts that best support us (see chapter 9, "The Higher the Thought"), our bodies will reflect this. A year from now we should be that much more vigorous and alive, our skin that much more radiant, our energy that much more dynamic. The aging process becomes the age*less* process through recognizing that it is not an arbitrary experience done unto us but something we co-create.

Examining our thoughts and beliefs, especially those we might have internalized years ago and are now ready to release, holds tremendous value. Doing this kind of internal housecleaning helps dissolve barriers to our connection with the divine. In *The Door of Everything*, Ruby Nelson's inspiring treatise on physical immortality, she writes, "Death came into existence, along with all the unhappy experiences, as a result of your misthinking." That is, death was created the instant we first thought of ourselves as separate from God. We need to learn (or relearn) that we are *one* with God. In the brilliance of that truth, we will undo the force of death.

Chapter 3

Breaking the Chain

THERE ARE PROBABLY VERY few people, including ordained clergy, who would not concur that most religions have had questionable beginnings or, at the very least, gone through periods in which their purpose and related practices were less than honorable. Whereas the Bible is often quoted as "the word of God," I say, "Who wrote it?" Although much of it might have been divinely inspired, the books of the Bible were nonetheless the works of men.

The Old Testament is rife with examples of a remarkably uncaring and vengeful—even sinister—God, a God willing to destroy persons on the wrong side of a dispute and a God not above asking Abraham, a father, to sacrifice Isaac, his son. But for all its flaws and misuses, there are still many great truths to be found in its pages. It tells us that we have been created in the image and likeness of God. Maybe we are even more like God than we've been told, and our assignment is to recognize this.

As presented in the stories of the New Testament, several miracles performed by Jesus involve his helping persons maintain or return to earthly life. And on at least one occasion, he made a direct verbal reference to experiencing life without death. In the gospel according to Saint John, he is quoted as saying, "Whosoever lives and believes in me shall never die" (John 11:26). Although traditionally interpreted as a reference to eternal life *after* death, perhaps there was an even more profound meaning to his statement, one that we have collectively ignored or misconstrued.

In allowing for the fact that we die, many religions have concocted ways to get it to jibe with their teachings. At some point in our personal evolution, if what we've been taught is no longer acceptable, we must be willing to challenge it, regardless of what the left hemisphere of our brain may tell us. The only way a negative situation can be changed is by admitting that it doesn't work, even if we have no idea what *will* work. It takes nerve to say it doesn't make sense that God wants us to age, get sick, and die. But why should we accept a less-than-perfect God? Religions are man-made cultural systems and are not necessarily aligned with what's best for us. For centuries, we have been ruled by the guilt and fear that they have generated. Of course, the parts of these religions that foster doing good work in the world are to be respected, but the problem becomes a pragmatic one when we try to define "good." Apparently, for some self-identified Christians, doing good means deterring others from their realization of self, particularly when that realization falls outside the parameters of their own Christian creed.

Isn't it time we take responsibility for the state of our existence? We have raised our eyes to heaven too often, beseeching help for circumstances we ourselves have created, expecting God to magically undo them. Is it possible that God also exists within us and that reaching outward has been effort put, literally, in the wrong direction?

It is through the tacit following of rote teachings for the masses that we have gently sauntered into oblivion. We can instead challenge convention and refuse to comply. Be forewarned that in so doing you will be subjecting yourself to ridicule. And even if the outside voices are mute, you may still have the internal thought, "If I take a chance at physical immortality and don't make it, I will look foolish." But what's the alternative? To proclaim with certainty that you are heading to your grave?

Many years ago, I took a tour of a Mormon church. It included a film presentation on how their bible came into existence. At its conclusion, I asked the woman serving as the guide if she knew why they called their bible the word of God. "Wasn't it written by men?" I asked. After hemming and hawing a bit, she said, "The truth is, I don't know." I appreciated her honesty.

Never refrain from questioning someone else's truth. It is only through challenging commonly held opinions and beliefs that we edge toward greater truths. It was once deemed virtuous for holy men to think in terms of "an eye for an eye." Then came the message of forgiveness and redemption. Now comes a time when people are saying we do not have to die to achieve eternal life. Our spirit, mind, and body can be resurrected living right here on earth. The barrier between God and humankind is one that we ourselves have created. Preachers eagerly tell us God's definition of good and evil, right and wrong, obligatory and prohibited. But your power can only come from owning your own truth. Whereas teachers, gurus, and sages may offer us guidance, it is the God within, accessed in stillness and quietude, that answers our questions.

I recently perused the contents of a spiritually oriented self-help book that included a chapter on death entitled "Death Is God's Will Too." I wonder if the author really believed that, or had she simply accepted death as an immutable fact of life and therefore searched for a way to justify it. Throughout the twentieth century, priests in the Roman Catholic Church, during its annual ritual known as Ash Wednesday, customarily told congregants, "To dust you shall return." Though not knowingly on their part, by denying the wellspring of life within them, participants in those ceremonies were passively pledging their allegiance to death. If we choose to exalt death over life, then dust is surely what we will become.

Personally, I have come to accept a good and benevolent God, a God that wants me to live. This was not always the case. Having been raised Catholic, I was not only taught that I had to die but that I would have to suffer after my death as well, for some indeterminate amount of time, in purgatory. Worms would inhabit my belly and fires consume my skin. And if I had committed too great a sin during my lifetime and God could not find it in his heart to forgive me, I would suffer for all eternity in hell. Fifty or so years ago, eating meat on a Friday was among such sins. It doesn't take a sage to see that these were the rants of the institutionalized ego gone mad. Perhaps the greatest harm of traditional religions has been in teaching us that we are sinners. We are no more sinners by nature than we are doomed by God to suffer and die.

We are equally prey to the chants of the individual ego. Just look at the discrepancy between the words of those who claim to understand the will of God and the way in which they live their lives. They allude to a time when they will "go home" and "be with God." Yet these are the very same people who are the first to profusely thank God, especially after recovering from a serious illness or accident, for saving them. From *what*? If their ultimate destiny and desire lie outside the physical body, why put off the paradise they claim so surely awaits them? Why not welcome death as the gateway to salvation? Indeed, is this not the message of many religions? "Oh, but my work on earth is not done yet," they might counter. Isn't it interesting that everyone's "work" is always completed within a hundred years? Is God so lacking in imagination that assignments never extend beyond that amount of time? The point is that *God does not kill people*. We kill ourselves with our thoughts.

Many traditional Christians believe in the resurrection of the physical body after death. In the fifteenth chapter of the First Letter to the Corinthians, there is the promise of the resurrection of the dead. But there is also a plea that, if realized, would circumvent that need relative to persons alive today. We are told, "For our perishable earthly bodies must be transformed into heavenly bodies that will never die. When this happens—when our perishable earthly bodies have been transformed into heavenly

14

bodies that will never die—then at last the Scriptures will come true" (1 Cor. 15:53–54). Could any of us aspire to a loftier goal?

That we are as essential to God's existence as God's existence is to us is a radical and, I'm sure, blasphemous idea to many. But that which we call God undoubtedly knows that each of us is an instrument through which its very essence is expressed, thereby making us indispensable. As we grow into spiritual magnificence, we will also perform miracles freely. With God (or Spirit) as the dominating force in our lives, we will no longer accept appearances as the only reality. We will know no limits. This is not arrogance but the deepest truth. We will also treat each other with greater kindness and respect, which, in turn, will help us create an as-yet-unimagined reality.

We have both willingly and unwittingly allowed the negative beliefs, fears, and biases of past generations to be an active part of who we are today. The mass consciousness of the human race has created situations that are intensely painful for many of us, and we have gone to great lengths to rationalize them, including misinterpreting the law of karma, the concept of reincarnation, and the promise of eternal life. But by examining our core beliefs, we take steps toward enlightenment, which is not something meant only for masters. It is our birthright. Indeed, it is the very reason we are here—to learn that which is necessary for the emancipation of our spirit. God asks little of us. If we are asked anything, it is to focus our attention and demonstrate our faith. Both mind and heart are essential for the transformation of our mortal beginnings into immortal splendor. When our thoughts and emotions are positive and passionate, the potential for transformation is unparalleled.

Chapter 4

Establishing the Connection

A DIVINE UNIVERSAL PRESENCE permeates all living things. This presence keeps us alive. Learning to connect with it in profound and deliberate ways is the key to our immortality. But the voice of God is gentle and needs a space in which it can be heard. In the course of a busy day, our internal guidance can get sidetracked. Spirit is with us every second of our existence, protecting and guiding. Yet just as an insecure child would shy away from a punitive parent, we too, through our anthropomorphic projections, have become reluctant to ask for help, feeling somehow unworthy.

Establishing our connection with the divine is as uncomplicated as we want it to be. Again, the barriers between divine nature and human nature are self-created; we make the choice whether to see or to deny the glory and wonder inherent in all sentient beings. It's been said that only the pure of heart can perceive the full intensity of Spirit without being consumed by it. But our purity is achieved instantly through our willingness to be transformed. And it is through our transformation, which is as much our responsibility as our privilege, that we reveal God's grandeur by serving as an example for others.

One of the biggest challenges to our faith is our attachment to physical things. If we lost every material thing we owned,

16

would we be willing to start over? News reports in recent years have been replete with inspiring stories of resilient persons who lived through natural disasters and had no choice but to do just that. As we enter this new phase of human existence, it seems we are being asked to reevaluate our perception of reality. We're used to looking outside ourselves for answers, sometimes even while knowing they aren't there. The only place left to look is the one place we were sure was barren—*inside*. But we look within with a sense of faith, knowing that there is more to us than we had previously imagined.

Why should our transformation be any less remarkable than that of a tomato seed? Taken at face value, it looks like a useless speck. Given the right conditions, however, it blossoms into a hardy green vine bearing robust red fruit. For us as humans, the seed of our transformation is the soul. But just as the tomato seed needs soil, water, and sunlight, our soul needs a conducive attitude in mind and heart. How often have we let mundane earthly matters dictate what must be done before we can turn our attention to things spiritual? I'm reminded of the times when, while immersed in a creative project, I would feel the pull to rearrange desk drawers, go through a file cabinet, or get involved in document management on my computer. Perhaps not surprisingly, the greater the significance of the project, the stronger the pull.

Luckily, there are many ways to reconnect with Spirit. Prayer, meditation, chanting, affirmations, and rebirthing are all excellent means, to name a few. Anything that helps us stay centered and calm will remind us that we are here to manifest our godliness. And what better way to do that than by willingly aligning ourselves with our Creator? If you have the sense of an ethereal guide, an entity or being that works with you (and yes, it can be an angel), acknowledge that relationship and encourage its presence. It can only serve you.

In a world fueled by frenetic external activity, considerable strength can be found in being still. It replenishes the soul, allowing us to remember our spiritual essence. Consequently, we can more readily demonstrate integrity and grace when interacting with others. The value of spending quiet time alone on a daily basis cannot be overestimated. Just as a chaotic, noisy environment can inhibit our access to our higher self, a peaceful, quiet one can facilitate new perceptions and perspectives.

Reflect for a moment on the amount of time you spend alone and how you spend it. If you are alone on a regular basis, do you routinely give yourself permission to do nothing, or is that time fraught with subtle tensions and pressures? I often felt that I hadn't earned the right to relax. My critical self-talk went something like, "How can I rest when I haven't saved the world yet?" Even seemingly benign thoughts like, "I have to catch up on my reading," can diminish the quality of quiet time. But almost always, if the time spent alone is tranquil and heart-centered, you will feel refreshed afterward.

Let's take a brief look at some of the methods we can use to consciously establish a spiritual connection.

Prayer, the Art of Talking to God

Prayer is the most modest form of worship. Through this unassuming act, we recognize the greatness of our Creator and, simultaneously, our desire to communicate with it. Many people who pray regularly prefer praying in the same physical place, whether a favorite room or simply a favored chair. Others enhance their experience by creating an informal altar in their home, with spiritual and/or religious symbols to inspire them. Above all, you should feel comfortable, centered, and unhurried when praying. In a direct and unadorned way, speak your concerns and desires from your heart. Don't worry about the length of the prayer. The feeling behind the words is far more important than the actual words. I start each day with the simple prayer, "Please, God, help me to do good work." And though I have often erred along the way, I do believe my sincerity has been rewarded. Whereas the merit of praying for a Porsche could be debated, it is completely theologically sound to ask that the divine plan of one's life be made manifest. As I see it, the penultimate goal of human existence is to make our lives a living prayer, second only to transforming this world into paradise. After all, prayer is as much about what we convey through our actions, demeanor, and attitude as it is about the words we speak.

Meditation, the Art of Listening to God

Actor and comedian Lily Tomlin has a great line that goes, "Why is it when we talk to God, we're said to be praying, but when God talks to us, we're schizophrenic?" Aside from its obvious humor, it speaks to our uneasiness about listening to the voice of God. Meditation comes in many forms. Anything you do that aligns you more closely with your authentic essence is a form of meditation. We can derive great benefits from just being silent and still, especially in nature. A walk in the woods is a form of meditation, as is sitting and listening to relaxing music. Even focusing our thoughts while exercising can be a form of meditation. Stay mindful of the pace and pattern of your breathing when engaged in any kind of meditative activity, as it is directly linked to your ability to maintain a calm focus. Start small. Allow ten minutes a day for quiet time, whether or not you are actually meditating according to your understanding of the word. The road to serenity can be patchy, and meditation offers one of the clearest roadmaps for maneuvering upon it.

Rebirthing

Rebirthing is a psychospiritual approach to mind/body purification. Using client-centered dialogue, a gentle breathing process, and personalized affirmations as its essential tools, it can help identify and release restrictive thoughts and beliefs, while increasing vitality, peacefulness, and sense of direction. The rebirthing philosophy is as detailed as it is cogent. It has the following five key elements:

1. *Birth trauma.* The study of how a person's birth can influence the entirety of his or her life is a new and growing field. Mounting research suggests that the type of birth we had (e.g., premature, Cesarean, induced, breech), as well as the varying aspects of the pregnancy that preceded it, can affect how we view life and interact with others (see Sondra Ray and Bob Mandel's book, *Birth and Relationships*).

2. *Parental disapproval syndrome.* Healing the relationship we have or have had with our parents is crucial to living a complete and harmonious life. Most of us were wounded in one way or another by our experience of childhood and coming of age. But when the roots of our dysfunction run deep and relate directly to either or both parents, those relationships need to be examined to create the space for healing.

3. *Personal lies.* These are the highly charged negative beliefs we have about ourselves. They're called lies because they represent tightly held untruths. The most common one is, "I'm not good enough." We've all felt this at one time or another. We are a society fueled by comparisons, and there will always be ways in which we compare less favorably to others. But comparisons are always a trick of the ego, which thrives on finding ways to make us feel "less than." Instead of comparing ourselves to others, let's openly acknowledge the ways in which others have been blessed.

   If we search diligently enough (and it's worth the search), each of us can identify our dominant personal lie—the single most negative thought we hold about ourselves, the one that has most taunted us or held us prisoner. Two that ruled me for years were, "I'm a freak," and "There's something wrong with me," each of which came from having had a father with an untreated personality disorder, and the fear that I was similarly challenged. The first one kept me from seeing myself as attractive, the second kept me subjugated to the opinions of others. In fact, if I disagreed with someone, especially if it involved an angry, heated argument, all it would take is a condescending, "What's *wrong* with you?" from my opponent and instantly I'd be reduced to rubble. But as I have unraveled these lies over time, it has allowed me to take on some pretty unpopular notions and remain centered. It's fittingly ironic that I possess a strong belief in physical immortality, as surely many people would not only disagree with the idea but might also characterize it as abnormal or unsound.

4. *Unconscious death urge.* This is the part of us that wants to die. It seems we all have it to some degree or another. At some point, we must decide to what extent we want to *live.* Who among us has not done something that, upon reflection, not only didn't serve his or her best interests but actually proved to be self-endangering? At the extreme end of this spectrum is suicide. But we can be suicidal in much more subtle ways. Any time we deny ourselves the opportunity for happiness, we effectively kill our spirit—a form of self-destruction that can be nearly as deadly.

5. *Past lives.* If your personal belief system includes reincarnation, consider the possible effects that your past lives might exert on your present one. If you sense you are having difficulties that cannot be traced to something in your life as you know it today, a past-life regression therapist could prove helpful. Similarly, if you have a specific memory that you believe stems from a past life, it would be best to address it directly with a transpersonal therapist who specializes in that area.

Affirmations

Perhaps no metaphysical technique is as magical or confusing as that of affirmations. An affirmation is a short and simple statement of truth—a truth you would like to manifest, stated in the present tense as if it were *already* true. Metaphysics teacher and lecturer Louise Hay compares saying an affirmation to placing an order in the "cosmic kitchen." Although, as she humorously points out, immediately after we place the order we often want to know what's taking the chef (in this case, God) so long.

Affirmations work on two levels, the psychological and the metaphysical. Psychologically, they help condition our mind to accept the possibility of a greater idea. They can also bring up any unresolved issues surrounding that idea, issues that could interfere with its manifestation. On a metaphysical level, the energy behind these statements moves the ethers to form substance out of thought. Although typically spoken aloud, to garner the greatest benefit from affirmations, I recommend a handwritten rebirthing exercise known as the response column.

After mentally composing your affirmation, grab a pad and pen. Write the affirmation slowly and your mind will automatically respond with a thought, often negative, at least initially. So, for example, if you are unhappy at work, writing, "I now have my ideal job," will make apparent where you are stuck around this issue. After you write the affirmation, write the first thought or response that comes to mind (e.g., "It'll never happen," or "no way," or "impossible") directly below it. Then write the affirmation again, followed immediately by whatever new or repeated response comes up. You would then continue this process of affirmation/response, affirmation/response until the responses were either neutral or positive. Believe it or not, if you do it long enough, this tends to happen. You can also make a recording of an affirmation or series of affirmations in your own voice, which is an effective means of penetrating the subconscious. It is best to alternate saying them in the first and second person (e.g., "I, Linda, now have my ideal job. You, Linda, now have your ideal job.").

A Course in Miracles

Originally published in 1975, *A Course in Miracles* is a three-volume set of books that is now more commonly issued as one large book consisting of three discrete sections, entitled "Text," "Workbook for Students," and "Manual for Teachers," respectively. Although study groups to facilitate integrating the wisdom of this spiritual masterpiece are not hard to find, at its core it remains very much a self-study course designed to foster self-reflective awareness. The Course is what some would call a channeled work, in that the person who actually wrote (or "took down") the words, psychologist Helen Schucman, said they were dictated to her by an inner voice. What's more, she never claimed authorship of the work.

The books address major spiritual themes of human existence, such as the nature of God, the purpose of the body, the role of forgiveness, and the meaning of salvation. Not unlike other revered texts of that ilk, different persons have interpreted the Course differently. One thing is undeniable: It offers a wholly unique way to look at life. It also asks us to move beyond the comfort of perfunctory existence to seriously contemplate the world of our experience, our understanding of God, and our relationship to both. On a personal note, if I were asked to identify the single greatest example of wisdom ever put into written form, I'd answer simply, *A Course in Miracles*.

I usually suggest that it is best read backwards. By that I mean, start with the Manual for Teachers, then do the Workbook (consisting of 365 daily lessons), and lastly, read the Text. The reason for my suggestion has to do with the density of the material, with the Manual for Teachers being the least intricate and the Text requiring the most deliberate focus in that regard. Don't be put off by the word "teachers" in the title of the third section; in Course terminology, we are all teachers to each other.

Chanting

There have been numerous anecdotal stories of healings attributed to the beneficial effects of chanting. Many who practice Eastern traditions, particularly Hinduism and Buddhism, use chants as an instrumental part of their daily spiritual work. Chanting typically involves methodically repeating a mantra—a word or group of words considered capable of initiating transformation—aloud, often to a very specific but simple melody. One of the more potent mantras and chants is *Om Namah Shivaya* (also spelled *Om Namaha Shivaya* or *Aum Namah Shivaya*). Although it lacks a literal meaning, it translates roughly to, "Infinite wisdom, infinite intelligence, I bow to the God within myself."

Many recordings have been made of this particular mantra. My personal favorite is the one that Robert Gass created. In the liner notes that accompany his audio CD entitled *Om Namaha Shivaya*, he tells an interesting story. During the early days of the rebirthing movement, a member of Sondra Ray's team contacted him with a special request. Sondra wanted to know if he would be willing to produce a ninety-minute version of his previously released five-minute recording of this chant. She had been using that recording in an extended-play format during parts of her workshops, and participants were having remarkable healing results just from the very sound of it. In point of fact, those who ascribe to a mantra's healing ability believe that our cells become infused with the vibrational frequency inherent in the words themselves.

Aligning the Chakras

Chakra is a Sanskrit word meaning "wheel" or "spinning wheel." According to ancient Indian tradition, we have seven major spiritual force centers (or wheel-like vortices) within our bodies. They are located respectively at the base of the spine, in the pelvic area, in the region of the stomach (or solar plexus), in and around the heart, in the area of the throat, between the eyebrows (also known as the third eye), and at the crown of the head. Each chakra governs a different aspect of our being. Accordingly, if one or more is underactive or overactive, it can affect the way we show up in the world.

Using visualization techniques or concentrating on these areas while meditating can help bring them into alignment. The simplest exercise in that regard is to close your eyes and imagine a whirling wheel of light in the area of the body in which the chakra you want to influence is located. If visualizing colors is something you can do without difficulty, it is best to use the color associated with that particular chakra. Alternatively, sending "white light" to the area will suffice. Consider reading about the chakras in greater detail in books written specifically about them. A classic book on the subject, originally published in 1927 and simply entitled *The Chakras*, by C. W. Leadbeater, goes in and out of print but is worth finding. By way of a brief overview, a concise chart follows below, listing the seven major chakras, the corresponding symbolic location in the physical body, the color that activates each, and the respective aspects of life that each affects.

CHAKRA	PHYSICAL LOCATION	COLOR	GOVERNS
1st	Base of the spine	Red	Survival instinct, vitality
2nd	Pelvic area	Orange	Sexuality, creativity
3rd	Stomach area	Yellow	Emotions, personal will
4th	Heart area	Green	Kindness, benevolence
5th	Throat area	Blue	Self-expression, judgment
6th	Between the eyebrows	Indigo	Imagination, intuition
7th	Top of the head	Violet	Spirituality, divine purpose

When Laughter Heals

As creator and facilitator of a workshop called Humor and Healing, I've often been asked what one has to do with the other. There have always been two kinds of humor—the kind that is divisive and alienating and the kind that celebrates our humanness and joins our spirits. A critical factor in allowing us to access the latter type is self-acceptance. In a judgment-free environment, our childlike self can, without too much cajoling on our part, be beckoned to come out and play. As adults, our sense of wonder may not be as readily accessed as when we were children, but it is that much richer when tapped. Humor flourishes in direct proportion to our spontaneity. Engaging in a playful activity frees our creative spirit. Bolstered by that energy, we can then face almost any situation in a way that says, "Look at me, I'm human—and it's okay."

The door that opens to levity, however, is a revolving one that can easily leave us on the other side, cloaked in darkness. As with any natural resource, humor must be handled with the respect it deserves. Misused or in the hands of a villain, it can be lethal. As comedian and author Joan Rivers once remarked, "The only weapon more formidable than humor is a gun." On the other hand, this very quality—humor's fundamentally combustible nature—can be used to our benefit, to break chains and liberate. Still, the resulting freedom can be as fear-producing as it is freeing, especially when its byproduct is comfort or pleasure. As a workshop participant once commented, "I tend to stay away from the things that make me feel good." This is a mighty voice that is difficult to quell, but quell it we must if we are to heal.

Fortunately, even just looking for the humor in an awkward or painful situation can reveal previously hidden vistas and facilitate our appreciation of the joys and ironies of being human. Applied to our own life circumstance, some of the basic principles of comedy writing (e.g., deliberate exaggeration or the element of surprise) can expand our vision and broaden our perception. And from an expansive, aerial view, things look different. Shortcomings lose their sting, mistakes become opportunities, and imperfections are seen as part of the tapestry of life.

The Ascension Attitudes

Three key elements in the process of our transformation are love, praise, and gratitude, sometimes referred to collectively as "the ascension attitudes." As a part of everyday living, we may feel challenged when we hear a horrible story—watching the news on TV, for example—or witness something that shakes our faith. Those are the moments we should deliberately focus on the good in our lives, knowing that signs from above do not precede our faith but rather, follow it. The ascension attitudes can help us integrate that realization. Let's briefly look at each.

Love

Love comes in infinite varieties but almost always entails the highest form of caring, which often translates into putting the needs of another on the same level as our own. It is also the cohesive substance of the cosmos, holding everything together, bringing harmony and order where they seem to be missing. As we become more secure in our connection to Spirit, we feel less fearful, and our ability to love increases.

Praise

There are ample opportunities, just by looking at the wonders of the world around us, to practice praise. By praising what we see, we make clear to the universal intelligence permeating all life that we value its gifts and do not take them for granted. Practicing praise heightens our sense of observation, ensuring that we remain active participants in the creative process. It also helps us maintain a positive outlook, which is essential for feeling connected to Spirit.

Gratitude

Flowing naturally from love and praise, gratitude is our humble gift to the universe, one way of saying, "Life is good." What we bless multiplies. And thanking God for that which we experience is a good way to preserve our health. Start with your senses. Bless your ability to see, to hear, to smell, to taste, and to feel. There is no reason why our senses shouldn't get better with time if we appreciate them for what they are—the tools with which we demonstrate our divinity.

I also recommend making an annual end-of-year blessings list. As December draws to a close, make a list of the good things that occurred during the course of the year. Despite any less-than-fortunate events that might have transpired, if you consciously enumerate the positive changes, you're certain to feel gratitude for the ways in which your life moved forward that year.

Till the Soil

Though certainly a physical activity, there is something remarkably spiritual about getting one's hands dirty with the richness of earthly soil. Planting and gardening offer multifaceted rewards. Aside from the intrinsically calming nature of all things horticultural, the activity itself keeps us centered and present-moment focused. There's also something inherently healing and therapeutic about plants and gardens. They present an excellent opportunity for the active engagement of four of our senses (or all five, if we happen to be tending a fruit or vegetable garden at harvest time). As importantly, caring for greenery affords us the chance to demonstrate some of the noblest of human traits and qualities: to nurture, to protect, to be responsible, to be creative, and to foster growth.

Living in an urban area is no excuse not to get involved in nature. Most large cities have community gardens within their larger parks. In many cases, volunteers are needed to assist with raking, weeding, planting, watering, et cetera. Even overseeing the care of a single houseplant can yield significant benefits. During those moments our attention is completely focused on the task at hand, while simultaneously tending to the welfare of another living thing, in this case a seed, seedling, or plant.

Chapter 5

TRUTH: The Realization Underlying Temporal Healing

I F HISTORY TEACHES US anything, it is that whenever we move forward into the unknown, society balks. It's as if we were born with an internal equation that reads, "change = fear." It seems to be a common human response, generated for the most part by ego, to discredit or ridicule any new philosophy, especially one that pushes the limits of existing, accepted beliefs. Although we have evolved socially to where we no longer crucify or burn those who speak a different truth, we don't necessarily listen. In a culture that puts a high premium on conformity and fitting in, it takes a modicum of courage to buck the system.

The scientific and medical communities could easily dismiss the ideas presented in this book as nonsense. When contemplating or reviewing immortalist philosophy, keep in mind that it is largely conjecture—so far. Changing our beliefs, especially those that form our bedrock, requires a mind as tenacious as it is open. It is very easy to retreat into old ways of thinking, particularly if our new thoughts are not well received. Once you start sharing these ideas with others you can almost count on people saying things like, "Do you really believe you can live forever?" In her book *A Return to Love*, Marianne Williamson cautions against casually sharing our deeply spiritual thoughts with those who have not yet begun to understand such concepts. In a similar vein, it is futile to ask scientists to search for God. God lives outside of science—beyond it. Faith is born in the private quietude at the center of our convictions. Once you understand this, those coming from a place of intellect alone will not disturb your serenity. Their response is *their* response. Your responsibility is to understand and own your own truth.

When I first heard about physical immortality, it resonated with me because part of me thought, regarding the issue of aging and related illness culminating in a slow and painful death, "Why would God do this to its children?" It just didn't make sense that if we were truly loved, we would be called home (assuming that "home" is somewhere other than here) in that way.

Actually, I'm not telling the whole truth. The very first time I encountered the idea I was standing in a bookstore, reading Sondra Ray's book *Celebration of Breath*, which offers a concise distillation of the rebirthing philosophy. I had gone through my first few rebirthing sessions with positive results and wanted to learn more about the constructs behind it. When I hit upon the pages describing physical immortality, I was astounded. I thought, "This woman is nuts. She must have an ego the size of Cleveland." But in fact it was *my* ego I was warring with. Over the ensuing years, however, the more I practiced rebirthing and the more I read, the more I allowed for the truth behind it. The turning point for me came during a wet rebirth in a pool. As I lay on my back, supported by my rebirther, with only my nose and mouth not submerged, I touched bliss. In that moment I was able to fully embrace being alive, thinking, "Yes, there's no reason why life has to end, and there's no reason why paradise cannot be found right here on earth."

But coming to own it has been another story entirely. One thing you'll notice as you begin to allow for the idea that life need not lead to death is just how entrenched we are in the belief that it must. The preparation for death is everywhere, sometimes subtly, sometimes blatantly, but ever present. We need to safeguard against the untruths that others can inadvertently pass on to us. Early in my own process of assimilating the concept of physical immortality, starting a reading and discussion group centered on immortalist literature was my way of doing that.

The difference between understanding something on an intellectual level and owning it as one's personal truth is tremendous. During the writing of this book, I had the experience of testing my own beliefs on several occasions. I left my job in social services, a job with excellent benefits, so that I could devote my time to two creative projects, this book being one of them. Understandably, I was haunted by thoughts like, "What if it doesn't happen?" It is too simplistic to say, as a response to such thoughts, "Have faith." Doubts and insecurities will continue to surface until we are ready to give them up. So why do we hold onto them? Well, for one thing, we get to experience frustration and unhappiness, which are, if nothing else, familiar. And if one of our personal lies happens to be, "I'm not entitled to happiness," then we also get to prove that we're right.

When dealing with New Age disciplines, a word of caution is in order. It is not uncommon to read or hear accounts of astounding growth and transformation that occurred very swiftly merely by using some simple metaphysical practice, affirmations being one of the more common. And it is equally common to feel a frustrating sense of failure when we first try these techniques ourselves, but to no avail. It's important to remember that everyone's path is different and that what works for someone else might not work for you (and vice versa). One complaint I have about some self-help books with a metaphysical slant is that they are written in a heavy-handed manner, implying that these great truths should work for every person in every situation every time, including the first time. Whereas some disciplines can produce remarkable results within a short period of time, others can take years to master, and some may never be the right match for us. That we not fall into the trap of self-judgment is of equal import to any benefit we may reap.

As you read the various ideas in this book, stop periodically to reflect on what you're thinking and feeling. Again, our unconscious thoughts are just as powerful as our conscious ones. If a small inner voice is secretly or quietly whispering, "This is nonsense," you won't reap any practical benefit from the ideas shared herein. On the surface, there is every reason to believe that it is not possible to live forever, since no one has ever done it. Technically, no one will *ever* be able to do it, since "forever" will always be in the future.

In a sense, everything we learn is learned on two levels, first through our surface-mind and then, more significantly, through our heart-mind. The surface-mind is the stalwart keeper of the gate—an idiot savant of sorts, entrusted with guarding the castle that is our body, mind, and spirit. Its job is to keep what's inside in and what's outside out, and it does it very well. The single biggest barrier to assimilating any new thought is getting past this big lug, it not being particularly conscious or wise but to its credit, remarkably consistent. The heart-mind, on the other hand, more closely resembles Einstein by comparison.

Continuing with this analogy, inside the castle, the thought Death is Inevitable (which I'll call DI) is resting comfortably. Outside the gate is a visitor, new in town and not bad looking, named Physical Immortality (which I'll call PI). PI approaches the castle and gently but firmly tells the surface-mind, "I'm here to visit the heart-mind." "No [expletive] way," the surface-mind replies with its characteristic finesse. But PI is confident and takes rejection in stride; it knows not to judge by appearances. And so PI calmly responds, "I would appreciate the opportunity to look inside the castle. I don't need to stay." Now, the surface-mind is suspicious, but even within its limited capacity is nonetheless impressed with the tranquility, peacefulness, and radiant glow of PI. After hesitating awhile, the surface-mind reluctantly acquiesces, saying, "Okay, but make it quick."

Once PI has entered the castle, DI immediately senses something and feels threatened. You, as the owner of the castle, feel a bit ill at the prospect of having brought these two together. Without wasting any time, PI heads straight for the heart-mind to plead its case. The heart-mind listens, confused but receptive. DI, now furious and fast on the heels of PI, quickly intervenes and starts to rant. "I have ruled for centuries. I have been taught, passed down, and feared from generation to generation. How can you entertain a visit from an outsider the likes of this? Everyone sane, rational, and wise believes in me. I command you to dismiss this intruder at once!" The heart-mind ponders, hesitates, and then, sadly, agrees. It tells PI to leave, that there's no room for it in the castle. "Okay, as you wish," replies PI. "But do me one favor. Think about what I have said to you. And *then* forget me, if you can."

When we first encounter the concept of physical immortality, it's a little like getting bopped on the head with a velvet hammer. We might remark to ourselves, incredulously, "Imagine that someone could be stupid enough to believe it's possible to defeat death." But there soon comes a time when it haunts us into considering its implications, or we dismiss it completely and put it on the shelf for a decade or two. If you find yourself in the former category, it is my prayer that this book will spur you on to continue your own exploration (see the suggested reading list for other books on the subject).

Once the seed of truth is planted, it needs to be nourished by our thinking and cherished through our faith. Whereas the metamorphosis of a caterpillar into a butterfly is predestined, our evolution from mortal to immortal requires understanding, acceptance, and determination. When we encounter painful or distressing situations, we may be tempted to accept them as unavoidable or irresolvable. Instead, we must be vigilant (using what some call healthy denial) in knowing that there is nothing *in form* that cannot be changed through the combined power of Spirit and our thoughts. At any moment, a stressful circumstance can be turned around and undone by the same force that created us. We need to be particularly careful not to fall prey to the judgments of others when facing such challenges. If our vision isn't manifesting, there may be a good reason for it. We may not be ready, there may be something we need to learn first, or maybe on an unconscious level we don't even want it.

Truth is the most valuable commodity we can possess, even with as many varieties of truth as there are people. Our personal truth is the fount from which our healing springs; the more we understand and embrace it, the less the hold and influence of worldly utterances upon us. It is my experience that persons coming from an immortalist perspective are more appreciative of life and much more adaptable, partly because they recognize both the value and the whimsical nature of each moment. Without a rigid, fixed view of things, we can more readily manifest comfort, ease, and wholeness in our daily lives. If you allow your expanded consciousness to tell you that life is good and can be eternal, your sense of wonder is sure to increase.

Chapter 6

Mirror, Mirror

ALL OUR PHYSICAL EXPERIENCES begin life as a thought, concept, or idea. That is, the birthplace of all tangible manifestation in our own lives is our own consciousness. If we want insight into the deep-rooted personal beliefs that we often conceal from others, and sometimes from ourselves, we need only to look at our own experiences. Do we believe in sickness or health, poverty or wealth, sorrow or joy? The details of our life circumstances are the clearest indicator of our internal dialogue. Most of us operate from a position of, "I'll believe it when I see it." We want proof of something before we're willing to commit to it. Whereas this makes total sense to the workings of our logical mind, the laws of Spirit don't operate that way. Rather, we are asked to have faith first, believing that our needs will then be met. In metaphysical circles, the idea that the outer world is a reflection of our inner thoughts is commonly represented by the expression, "The world is our mirror."

Of all the New Age maxims, this is the trickiest to analyze, understand, or discuss. The ego has a field day with this one because it can so easily be misinterpreted or used to attack oneself or others. It's all too easy to point a finger at someone going through a rough time and think, "You must have accumulated some pretty heavy karma, pal." Or less accusatory but just as judgmental,

"You must have a strong belief in pain and misery." More to the point, we have no way of knowing the profound truth behind someone else's situation, such as whether they're experiencing something that can serve as a catalyst for their soul's evolution, as an inspiration for someone else in a similar circumstance, or simply as a lesson in humility. It is spiritually ignorant to reduce the complexities of another's life for the purpose of categorizing or dismissing their challenges.

The mirror principle affects all our relationships and is a precursor of the Golden Rule, in that it bids us to treat others with the same attention and respect with which we would like to be treated. Intimate, romantic relationships are no exception; your spouse is as much your mirror as anyone else in your life. He or she is there to help you learn more about yourself and to bring you closer to God, just as you play a similarly reciprocal role in his or her life. You'll also be less likely to judge your life partner if you recognize that he or she is reflecting back to you only that which already exists in you.

Although the human body is not the only temple for God, it is the one we are using now. And when we get sick, it is often because we have negated the vision of ourselves as whole and have conceded seeing ourselves as vulnerable or weak. Just as all illness is of the mind, all healing involves replacing fear with love, though often our fears are unconscious, including the fear of illness. In metaphysics it is known that any thought upon which we focus increases in strength and intensity. By putting mental energy into our fears, we help them materialize. We can instead put our energy into the things we'd like to manifest. If you want increased prosperity, keep your focus on wealth. Along similar lines, if you want to avoid a stroke, don't spend time obsessing over the odds of having one.

If we've created a negative situation, the only question to ask is, "What can I learn from this?" Great empowerment can be found in taking responsibility for what we see in front of us, for in that responsibility lies the ability to undo it. If we created it, we can uncreate it. If we find our world filled with people, or even one person, trying to exert power or control over us, we can look within to see where we ourselves might have been manipulative or controlling. Although it is true that, on some level, we have asked for everything we've received into our lives, both the "good" and the "bad," this is most often done unconsciously. Our soul cries out for lessons our heart would never seek. Of course, the voice of the ego instantly counters with shouts of, "How could you be so stupid?" But such self-talk is not productive and never life enhancing.

There was a period of several years in my life, immediately following a series of metaphysical experiences that put me on the path of spiritual questing, wherein I couldn't find a sense of meaning or purpose. I was floundering. Somehow I thought that since Spirit had touched me, God was now on my side and life would be easy, straightforward, and direct. Aside from the fact that my logic was faulty, I wasn't yet convinced that happiness was attainable. And that, in turn, was reflected in the life I was leading. Just as I was unfocused in my own life, the persons I attracted were unfocused in theirs: I wasn't doing what I wanted for a living, neither were they; I was financially challenged, likewise for them; I was uncomfortable with my sexuality, they with theirs; I was in an unsatisfying relationship, ditto for them.

Working in social services doing vocational counseling within underprivileged communities, I even started judging some of my clients as unmotivated and indolent. At that time I was employed at a rather poorly run agency where I had become quite unhappy. So I tried to see how the thoughts I was having about others might be a reflection of something in me. After pondering a bit, it seemed clear: Whereas my clients had had long histories of being dependent on government agencies, I had had substantial stretches during which I was reliant on family members; whereas they resented someone trying to force them off public assistance, I resented toiling in a work environment in which the only reward was a paycheck; just as some of them didn't want to work, part of me didn't want to work either.

Again, I'd like to point out that the mirror principle should never be used as an opportunity to judge oneself or others. What it offers is the chance to shine light where there may be darkness. It's also a doorway to growth and change. Once we ingest the information presented to us, our only responsibility is to get a sense as to the appropriate next step. In my own case, described above, it gave me the chance to see how I hadn't fully invited prosperity into my life but was instead clinging to a belief in scarcity. It was then up to me to use the techniques I had learned to jimmy that construct from my consciousness. Now, lest I sound too matter-of-fact or spiritually arrogant, I want to stress that just because we know that a particular issue needs to be cleared doesn't mean we can clear it right away. The only thing that knowing ensures is an easier focus in terms of where the work needs to be done.

We are continually in the process of creating in our lives, and the world graciously offers us a constant reflection of our thoughts. As you work more closely with metaphysical disciplines, you will find yourself making observations using the mirror principle more frequently. It is worth reminding ourselves that we are never alone, no matter how much we may feel at times that we are. And if we keep a watchful eye, our interconnectedness can be seen in every aspect of our lives, from the incidental (e.g., silently worrying about a situation for days, when a friend hands us a magazine that just happens to contain an article on that very topic) to the inestimable (e.g., with quantum physics telling us that the scientist affects the experiment just by viewing it). In the world of our experience, there is little denying our connection to one another.

Chapter 7

Tapping the Universal Mind

MANY GREAT THINKERS, SCIENTIFIC and metaphysical alike, have said there is a oneness to existence and that somehow, behind and beyond the illusion of life as we know it, we are all magically connected. A fundamental tenet of contemporary quantum physics as postulated by physicists David Bohm and John Bell, among others, holds that all particles of matter are interconnected, even down to the atomic level. Or, as stated in a lyrical quotation often attributed to early twentieth century astrophysicist Sir Arthur Eddington, "When an electron vibrates, the universe shakes." Put another way, there is a field of intelligence within which all things, animate and inanimate, exist. This universal intelligence connects each of us to each other in ways we've yet to fully understand. The theory becomes evident in the way we all, at our very core, crave the same thing—happiness. Happiness is the carrot that motivates all of us. We don't want to win the lottery to become rich; we want to win because we believe the money will bring happiness. Those who seek fame do not seek it for fame's sake but for the happiness they think will come as a result of its attendant privileges.

As a collective universal mind, we are still quite infantile. We are just beginning to understand the ways of the psyche and the roots and seeds of our behavior. Many of us have marveled at

40

the seeming coincidence of phoning someone we haven't seen in years and hearing them say, "I can't believe you're calling me—I was just thinking about you yesterday!" But how often have we touched another's life without ever learning that we've done so? Healing does not happen apart or alone; we affect people in ways we can't even imagine. We extend what we think is a simple courtesy to someone, and the course of their life changes. One of the beautiful ironies of spiritual living is that it is through the act of trying to heal our own life that we positively impact the lives of others. When we demonstrate peace for ourselves, we not only set an example, we also create subtle opportunities, in the place where thoughts exist, for others to do the same.

According to the essential premise behind a theory of metaphysics known as the hundredth monkey, it is entirely possible that embracing physical immortality as an option for oneself can have an effect on persons who never even heard of the concept. The theory stems from a story that may be as much folklore as fact. It is nonetheless fascinating as a concept.

On the Japanese island of Koshima during the early 1950s, a colony of monkeys was supplied with sweet potatoes from a group of scientists. One of the young female monkeys, named Imo, started washing her potatoes in the shore's water and subsequently taught the technique to her mother and some of the other young monkeys. For a period of approximately the next six years, the number of monkeys that washed their potatoes grew very slowly, confined mostly to the younger monkeys and a select group of older monkeys that learned the technique from their offspring. Then one day the scientists noticed that virtually every monkey on the island had adopted this practice. That is, once a certain number of monkeys (arbitrarily referred to as "one hundred") were washing their potatoes, the idea rapidly spread from mind to mind and they all started doing it. More curiously, it was discovered that, at about the same time, monkeys on neighboring islands also started washing their potatoes. This makes a strong case for the idea that thoughts are tangible things. When the thought that it was best to wash their potatoes gained enough mental mass among the minds of monkeys living on Koshima Island, it was able to cross the water to other islands. We, as humans, are all on the same island, so to speak. Most people still adhere to the belief that death is inevitable, but fortunately not all. There is a movement afoot. I ask you to consider joining the wave.

We need to support each other in our vision of longevity. When enough of us begin to question the inevitability of death, we will witness something startling. People will start living to ages well beyond one hundred, maintaining excellent health and all of their faculties. And when enough people view that achievement as "no big deal," there will be a shift in perception—the very definition of a miracle according to *A Course in Miracles*. It would then be considered odd or atypical when someone dies *before* the age of one hundred.

Unfortunately, because of the way the laws of metaphysics work, unless a certain number of people—our human equivalent of the simian one hundred—start believing that they are immortal, it will not manifest as reality. We must fully acknowledge how dependent we are on each other for salvation. Truth does not happen in a vacuum; rather, it is something we create together. When skeptical friends ask me, "Ed, if you die, does that mean you were wrong?" I usually respond, "No, it means that not enough people were willing to join me in my vision." For it is a certainty that it cannot be done alone.

One advantage to recognizing how we are all connected is that it allows us to tap into each other's wisdom as a resource. If someone else has a brilliant thought, *you* benefit. Our collective knowledge (known, in some spiritual teachings, as the Akashic Records) is stored in the universal unconscious. We are constantly sharing thoughts on an unconscious level. As our understanding of the mechanics governing this process evolves, we will become progressively more proficient in this domain. When we feel challenged, we can ask the universe for help and know that a solution will be revealed to us. This is where intuition comes in.

Borne by our shared thoughts, intuition forms a pipeline to the universal mind. You can probably recall a time when you had a strong visceral feeling telling you not to do something. The genesis of your feeling might well have stemmed from the wisdom garnered by someone else, when they were in a similar situation. Their experience, now a permanent part of their life, is also now a part of the universal mind.

Learning to tap into this universal wisdom becomes easier with time. Becoming conscious of it—that is, remembering to listen for it—is the first step. Accessing it is the root of creative genius. All truly great works, be they scientific, artistic, or political, arise from within this universal intelligence and are then channeled outward into the world through our individual personalities. A practical side effect of using this intelligence is that it enlivens our bodies, allowing more life to flow through us. And this, in turn, is reflected in both our physical and mental well-being.

Chapter 8

The Palace of the Ego

UNTIL OUR THOUGHTS AND actions have been cleared to the point where we can serve as a constant channel for Spirit, we are subject to the dictates of the ego—and physical immortality will remain elusive. I'm the first to admit that it does not always seem possible. Negative, fear-based thinking is the way of the world and we are all susceptible to it. But beliefs in limitation are just our own resistance to the inherent goodness of life. Limited thinking obscures our vision and doesn't allow for a reality beyond that which we've already created. It's also why we tend to define the world in terms of its problems rather than its possibilities. If our surface-mind is full with unloving and judgmental thoughts, we can't receive new or better ones. We discard clothing when it no longer fits or feels right. Well, we are just as clothed in our thoughts as we are in our garments, and it is just as necessary to release those that no longer fit or feel right.

One thing is readily apparent about negativity—it spreads, it propagates. It is resourceful, virulent, and will find its way into any situation in which it is allowed. It therefore becomes our duty to keep it out. Negative thoughts and images are best stopped at their inception. When we feel the pull of a negative thought, we can consciously redirect our attention to something positive. We can start by monitoring what we think and say to ourselves. How often, during the course of a day, do you find yourself thinking thoughts like these: "Why bother?" "It doesn't matter." "What are the odds?" "Who cares?" "It'll never happen." "What's the use?" Left unchecked, these kinds of thoughts mushroom like moldy spores in dank places.

A friend once told me that in moments of fear, anxiety, and self-doubt, when plagued by feelings of unworthiness, his response is a simple one—a mantra, repeated over and over, that simply goes, "No ego." That's it. *No ego.* Many of our existing limitations are *perceived* limitations stemming from this unhealed part of the psyche and the veil it creates. The ego lives very much in a world of its own creation. Its currency is Ego Dollars, issued and redeemed in Ego Land. In its endless effort to prove itself right, the ego will go to great lengths to validate and rationalize the existence of something it cannot understand. It is our attachment to the ego that keeps us from knowing and demonstrating our heart's desire. Paradoxically, releasing ourselves from the ego's grip allows us to realize a greater sense of self and lead a fuller life. You can usually sense when someone is coming from ego. Thankfully, although Spirit is not visible, it is nevertheless palpable. We can feel it, and our heart can tell when someone is aligned with it.

Any time we doubt our own worth, some part of our God-stuff escapes. I'd like to see a pin or button made that reads, "Keep Doubt Out." It's not arrogant to recognize and appreciate our own greatness, as long as we acknowledge its source. Loving yourself unconditionally can even eliminate chronic physical pain. Now, a statement like that can be misinterpreted as meaning that the suffering individual is somehow to blame for their pain. They are not. Because even though we co-create our own reality, most of us are not even aware that we do it, let alone *how* we do it.

Are you quick to anger? Do you harbor feelings of resentment? Are you carrying past hurts into the present, things that need to be released? Make a commitment to let go of that which no longer serves you. One way of doing this is by using a simple forgiveness exercise.

Think of someone you need to forgive. Get a pad of lined paper and, starting at the top, write, "I, [your name], now forgive [their name] completely, for everything." Write the sentence, slowly and repeatedly, until you have filled the page with it. As you do this exercise, pay careful attention to the emotions that surface, which may surprise you. They will help you uncover the elemental truth behind the aspect of that person's behavior that you found offensive or hurtful. This kind of forgiveness work, though rudimentary, can be utterly transformative.

We all have ideas as to how things "should" be. And when those values and beliefs are challenged, we sometimes get angry or try to escape. Escape can take many forms. Some are obvious (work, food, or alcohol), some less so (commiserating with a friend or going to the cinema). How many of us have found ourselves at the movies when we should have been home writing one? So how has your ego tricked you? By this I mean, what is the one thing you believe would, if it were different, make your life harmonious? I often felt that if I were truly wealthy, there would be many things I wouldn't have to deal with, and my life would therefore be easier. But in point of fact, most of the skills and abilities that I have unearthed in my own life have come as a result of my efforts to discover ways in which I could earn money in accordance with my personal values. Healing the money issue forced me to heal issues I might otherwise have avoided or overlooked.

Think of a situation that has bothered you, something you can't get beyond, a place where your ego has you hooked. Now take an aerial view. Look at the big picture—the bigger, the better. Go outside yourself to consider what this person, incident, or occurrence means or might have meant to someone else. If you are hurt because of someone else's behavior, see it through their eyes. They were most likely scared, confused, or fearful. This is not said by way of condoning bad behavior. It is too easy to use metaphysical principles to become passive and silent for fear of appearing non-spiritual. All the same, if there is only one great truth, one universal mind—that is, if there is, in effect, only one "person" in the universe with each of us a reflection of each other, what do we stand to gain by holding onto our hurt feelings?

One of the most expedient and direct ways to release negativity is through the use of a rebirthing dialogue process, a sentence completion exercise designed to identify our dominant personal lie (see chapter 4, "Establishing the Connection"). For the purpose of illustrating this technique, I will re-create here a simulated dialogue between rebirther and client. The rebirther initiates the process by asking the client to complete the following two sentences: "The most negative thought I have about life is _____," and "The most negative thought I have about myself is _____." Let's look at each.

1. The most negative thought I have about life is ...

Rebirther: The most negative thought I have about life is ...
Client: Life is unfair.
Rebirther: The way in which life is unfair is ...
Client: I can't get what I want.
Rebirther: The reason I can't get what I want is ...
Client: There's too much competition.
Rebirther: The problem with competition is ...
Client: I can't compete.
Rebirther: The reason I can't compete is ...
Client: I don't deserve to win.

At the conclusion of this process, the rebirther creates the following affirmation for the client: *I am now fully capable and deserving of winning.*

2. The most negative thought I have about myself is ...

Rebirther: The most negative thought I have about myself is ...
Client: I hate myself.
Rebirther: The reason I hate myself is ...
Client: I'm not productive enough.
Rebirther: The reason I'm not productive is ...

Client:	I'm afraid.
Rebirther:	The thing I'm most afraid of is …
Client:	Rejection.
Rebirther:	The hardest thing about experiencing rejection is …
Client:	Not being accepted for who I am.

At the conclusion of this process, the rebirther creates the following affirmation for the client: *I now love and accept myself, exactly as I am, in all situations.*

After doing your own mental housecleaning, you may want to take a look at your friends and family. Those closest to us may outwardly claim to be supportive, but upon closer inspection it's sometimes less clear. Though often largely unconscious on their part, if you listen closely to their words, you will uncover their core beliefs. So, for example, if the favorite expression of someone you love is, "Life is short," or "At my age, I'll never be able to [fill in the blank]," you may want to consider the effect that their ideas are having on you. Some people are in a committed relationship with negativity. I have a friend with whom I was once much closer than I am today. One reason? Each time we got together she would, at some point during our visit, lament, "I'm getting older, I'm getting older." I tried pointing out that this was an affirmation, a negative one, but an affirmation nonetheless. Her response? "But I am!" Some people's thoughts and beliefs are so tightly clenched that other greater ones cannot get through. This friend and I still see each other on occasion, though we don't connect in the way we once did. On an energetic level, it follows logically that as our personal evolution progresses, we tend to let go of persons whose energy no longer supports who we are, or who we're becoming, to make room for those who do.

For me the challenge of all challenges is one I might refer to, diplomatically, as the "difficult" personality. We've all had the experience of going forth into the day feeling centered, well-grounded, and confident, only to be accosted by an "a-hole." Whether we like to admit it or not, we have complete control over how we react to other people. And so the question becomes, just how much of our power do we want to give away? If someone is rude to you, and you are not in touch with this basic metaphysical truth, you may find yourself thinking, "That bastard ruined my day." A more accurate description would be, "I let that person rob me of my peace." Upon thoughtful reflection, we can see that such persons are usually hurting and merely playing out their own "stuff." Granted, it may feel as if we have stumbled upon a person whose stuff is surely meant for someone else. But if we are committed to the maxims, "We create our own reality," and "There are no accidents," this individual provides an opportunity for us to demonstrate our own level of awareness. But again, where this gets tricky is in not letting people abuse us. It's one thing to understand the root of someone's rudeness; it is quite another to let it go unacknowledged or unchallenged. Protecting oneself often means taking appropriate action.

I have not personally reached the point where my buttons can't be pushed. Ironically, sometimes the less important the incident, the more troubling the feeling. Not long ago, while riding a commuter train, I decided to change my seat and moved from one car to another. Looking for a place to sit, I walked past the conductor in the car that I had just stepped into. "Let me see your ticket!" he rudely snapped in an abrupt staccato. "Sure," I said but continued to walk, thinking I would first find a seat upon which to rest the bags I was carrying. "Let me see your ticket NOW," he bellowed. My instant gut reaction was anger—intense, vitriolic anger. My thought was something on the order of, "Who do you think you are?" I showed him my ticket, said nothing, and took my seat.

So the question remains, how does one deal with persons who are inappropriate? We can begin by recognizing that the opposite of love is fear. Someone whose actions are less than loving is very likely masking, whether consciously or unconsciously, his or her own hidden fears. *A Course in Miracles* tells us that the "miracle" (that is, the kind, loving gesture) is extended from one who is temporarily more "sane" to one who is temporarily less so. In the preceding scenario, the best I could do was to ignore the conductor. I wasn't "sane" enough to extend love at that moment. When confronted with what we view as harshness or lack of feeling on the part of another, if we could see their actions through the lens of their experience, we might see that what they are doing is attempting to shield themselves from perceived vulnerability and harm. Ironically, it is this same unwillingness to address internal fears that, through projection, creates external stressors. We tell each other it's a cold, cruel world and then expect that we will somehow embrace it. How could we? Why *would* we?

The unbridled sports fan demonstrates another example of the ego at play. I'm referring here to the over-the-top histrionics exhibited most typically by male fans when they are psyched for a particular team, player, or event. I suppose we could call it exuberance personified and leave it at that. But at the root of it is an ego nearly as disconnected from Spirit as that of an abusive spouse. If we look at the tone, stance, and bearing of a screaming male fan, the key elements are rage and objectification. It's about venting his frustration, demonstrating his idea of maleness, and getting what he wants. The team member (or the team itself) becomes a substitute for what he perceives as missing from his own life. Since he is not viewed as an athlete or a hero, he gets vicarious recognition and satisfaction by grabbing onto the coattails of someone who is. The sports fanatic, vexed by the ways in which he may feel ineffective, transfers his ferocity to his favorite player or team. It's also a socially acceptable way of embracing his need to bond with other men without displaying overt affection.

Most sporting events have, at their foundation, the idea of someone or something being better than another—a winner and a loser. This is but another invention of the ego. God doesn't care which team wins a ballgame. The fan gives the team the magical power to bestow honor and worth upon its spectators. But, you see, we are *already* worthy.

So what does it mean to surrender the ego? What does it

mean to give one's life completely to God? Firstly, it means taking responsibility for the life we are presently leading, as it exists today. It also means acknowledging that a unifying presence guides and directs us at all times. We can easily get caught up in the seeming reality of everyday life and forget about God. But if we haven't dedicated our day to this healing universal essence, we aren't really doing anything at all. We may exist; we might even be living, but it is a life bereft of passion and purpose. Conversely, there is a certitude that is undeniable and clear when we view the world with God's eyes. We then see it through the lens of forgiveness, compassion, kindness, and respect.

Chapter 9

The Higher the Thought

TO ANY GIVEN SITUATION, we have the opportunity to respond in a multitude of ways. Since form follows thought, choosing the highest possible thought allows us to respond in the highest possible way. In her audio recording entitled *Lasting Love Relationships*, Sondra Ray defines the highest thought as that which is "the most positive, the least limiting, and the most productive." Let's look at each element individually.

The most positive

A positive thought produces a positive result. Plainly put, that which is positive is that which is in our best interests. And it is in our best interests to survive. There is no more essential thought than that. I challenge anyone who believes in the existence of God to tell me that He/She/It has decreed old age and death to be part of a master plan. What loving parent would want His/Her/Its children to experience what is typically referred to as "the natural aging process"?

The least limiting

That which is not in line with the infinite limits our potential. Whenever we limit our beliefs, we deny the majesty of our Creator. We are not limited in any way except by that which we affirm. Many of us have internalized the idea that to accept ourselves unconditionally is to be flagrantly arrogant or egotistical. But there is a way of being that allows for knowing our selfhood and owning our greatness that is not ego-based. It comes from understanding the force behind our creation and our very existence. Let's commit to not believing in limitations, neither those others have imposed, nor those we have created for ourselves.

The most productive

That which is in line with the infinite produces glorious results. It bears fruit. We can welcome each day knowing we are part of God's design and that our input is essential to the beauty and wonder of life. This means accepting that we are not idle thoughts in the mind of God but are instead its creations and, as such, rejoice in having a function, mission, and purpose.

When we come from a place of grounded spirituality we can more readily look for the highest thought in any given situation, which, in turn, brings about the most peace. When we are peaceful, we feel safe; when we feel safe, we want to live; and wanting to live helps keep us alive. Yes, living entails challenges and discomfort. But in order for us to entertain the concept of an unending life, that life needs to be more comfortable than uncomfortable. The only way we'll ever have lasting harmony is if everyone—and I mean everyone—feels safe, peaceful, and content. There is lyrical symmetry in realizing that we cannot save ourselves alone. Fortunately, combining our efforts decreases our sense of oppression just as it increases our sense of personal responsibility. As a natural result, we stop blaming outside forces (individuals, groups, or organizations) for our circumstances or our fate.

Many worldly problems are the result of our not collectively seeking and applying the highest thought to a situation. It is a generally recognized fact that there's more than enough food on the planet to feed everyone. Indeed, according to the World Food Programme, the world's largest humanitarian organization fighting hunger on a global level, "There is enough food in the world today for everyone to have the nourishment necessary for a healthy and productive life." And yet, children go to bed hungry. Most wars, begotten over territorial disputes and/or conflicts about religion, are an extension of the belief that one country, sect, or group has a handle on the truth. As we expand our consciousness to allow for broader, wider spanning beliefs, our eagerness to get people to see things *our* way diminishes. When faced with a new or better way to think, some people are reluctant to consider it for fear of appearing indecisive or lacking in personal command. But being flexible doesn't discredit our ability to stand by our principles. It merely means that our ability to receive and review new information is intact.

If the general speculation that we use only one-tenth of our brain is correct, we probably also use only one-tenth of our soul, with nine-tenths of it below our conscious awareness. Sometimes called the submerged mind or the heart-mind, it has never entertained or engendered a negative thought. When mind and heart work together, the resulting alchemy is powerful. But instead of harnessing the incredible gifts proffered by this duo when they work in tandem, we have chosen to use each in ways that do not serve us. In essence, by focusing on the illusory parts of life, we have magnified illusion. Given the chance, our ego will take the tiniest seed of negativity—the ordinary concern that surfaces when awaiting a test result, for example—and blow it into a full-fledged disaster. Not on a conscious level, of course, since consciously almost everyone would choose that which is in his or her best interests. But what about the unconscious? On that level, we have not learned how to resist negativity. It's not anyone's fault; we just haven't.

In my perception, higher thought encompasses helping others realize their identity and their calling. As we come to value our neighbors as much as we value ourselves, we will naturally want to support them in achieving their dreams. Without dreams, life is drudgery. Because many of us hold an ingrained belief in scarcity, we often look at others and see their attainment of success as in some way impinging upon our own, as if there is only so much "good" to go around. Quite to the contrary, it is through sharing and giving that our own bounty multiplies. The more we give from our heart and our spirit, the more we receive. But there is a catch. We first must be willing to accept good into our own lives. How many of us were raised to believe that abundance, prosperity, and wealth are somehow ungodly?

Loving others means supporting them in reaching their goals and in becoming all that they can. There is a delicate art to knowing when to put another's needs first. Still, it is possible to be fully there for others while honoring our own needs. We can also support each other in ways that take virtually no time. When we pray for someone else we enhance that person's spiritual essence, and that takes literally seconds. I'm a great believer in the five-second prayer. Saying or thinking, "Bless [person's name], God," takes less than five seconds but demonstrates to our Creator and ourselves that we are thoughtful, caring beings who are there for each other. And that's the point, really. Certainly God doesn't need to be reminded as to whom among us needs help at any particular moment. But broadening our individual awareness to include those in need helps expand our collective consciousness. And that, in turn, changes lives.

As a society, we tend to shun that which threatens or scares us. Many of us keep our distance from older adults because we believe they are close to death, and death is a scary proposition for most of us. But if aging is not an automatic process independent of our thoughts, we can begin to think differently about what growing older means. And yet, confidence does not mean control. We can gain personal mastery over our lives but still recognize that life is so broad in scope that we cannot predict what is coming. We can, however, predict how we would respond to what might come our way.

By way of example, heart disease is common in my family, especially among males. And so I made an agreement with myself not to dwell unduly upon the subject. However, when applying metaphysical principles to one's physical health, the ego can fool us in ways we weren't anticipating. We live in a physical universe, guided by physical laws, yielding physical consequences; hence, these kinds of decisions require deep personal reflection and introspection. I could have told myself, "I've already prayed about it, and since God is aware of my needs, there's not much else to do—and yes, I'd like fries and a milkshake with that cheeseburger." That would be little more than shirking personal responsibility. Instead, I choose to make proactive choices that support the health of my heart, including reducing my intake of saturated fats, exercising regularly, and taking a cholesterol-lowering agent. But I also turn my focus away from the problem, heart disease, and keep it squarely on the desired result, heart health.

So what's the highest thought one can choose on the subject of aging? Consider the following: If you are an active, healthy individual, at what age will you become old? Or at what age will it start? These are important questions to ponder because most people have an age in mind, but it is usually in the *back* of their mind, where it can do a lot of harm. For some it's forty, for many, it's fifty, after which they are no longer young. I am inviting you to stay young by abolishing the belief in an age beyond which you can no longer be defined as such.

Now that people are living longer than ever before in history, the number of research projects examining the lives of centenarians is growing. One of the more recent studies, entitled "Images of Ohio Centenarians," conducted by Lisa Groger and Jessie Leek, cited the following among their key findings: "Age was not salient for the participants in our study. They acknowledged their age but confessed to not thinking much about it. They were busy living in the present." As has often been lauded, and as this study attests, the value of living in the present cannot be overly emphasized.

If you live life one day at a time—truly one day at a time, you will see how easy it is to believe in eternal youthfulness. When you go to sleep tonight, ask yourself if you expect to wake up old tomorrow. Of course, the answer is no. So on which tomorrow *would* you wake up old? To which you might respond, "No, stupid, it doesn't work that way. It happens slowly, over time, so slowly we don't see it happening." That is exactly the problem. It happens slowly enough so that we don't notice it. But by bringing our conscious awareness to it, the process changes. However, the societal view of remaining consciously aware of age is something else entirely.

We seem, at least in the United States, very much an age-centric society, preoccupied with age for age's sake. Most television news reports on persons in the public eye, such as sports or entertainment figures, will usually mention their age as part of the story. When a famous person is written about in print media, their name is often followed by a comma, which in turn is followed by their age. This practice of routine age disclosure is not limited to celebrities. It's also very common to give the age of any person who happens to be the focus of an item covered during that city's evening news broadcast. Their age is often even included in the teaser used to promote the program: "57-year-old woman from Astoria held at gunpoint in local pharmacy. Tonight at eleven." This kind of incessant reminder of the number we carry, in a culture that is far from immortalist, cannot help but make us think about our own chronological age vis-à-vis where we fall on the continuum, all the while believing that the greater the number, the closer our proximity to death.

Now, what about persons who are already elderly and infirm? You know, the ones that comedians Tim Conway and Carol

Burnett spoofed on her television show. Unfortunately, many older adults who are now feeble and frail had several disadvantages during their early and middle years. They lived during a time when we were unaware of the roles that diet, exercise, and stress played in aging. More significantly, it was a time when people didn't question authority. They blindly deferred to what they were told. And everyone *knew* that people grew old. The image of the old person bent over from age was simply accepted as a fact of life. And since form follows thought, grow old they did.

But not anymore.

I have long believed that where there is life, there is hope. Even a person experiencing the ravages of the collective beliefs about aging that have been passed down from generation to generation can undo at least some of their effects by thinking differently.

When someone knocks your belief in your ability to achieve physical immortality, stop and think for a minute. Is his or her thought coming from a godly place? Or would the mind of God be more in line with your desire to live? Though not one of us knows where the vast mystery of life will lead, it seems safe to say that wherever it takes us, getting there by choosing life would be the higher road.

Change really does happen one person at a time. Each of us can make a difference by speaking our truth and refusing to hide. Skepticism and ridicule almost certainly await us from those who cannot fathom the idea of dramatic longevity. But so what? We are not living life for the sake of receiving validation from others. As more and more persons say yes to the possibility of physical immortality, we will see a noticeable change in the social and cultural values held around aging. It takes but a few voices to broach the subject with some seriousness for others to take note. As the number of minds embracing this idea continues to grow, we will witness many major changes. What joyous wonders await us here on earth, if we will only bid them welcome.

Given that the title of this chapter is "The Higher the

Thought," it seems fitting to conclude with my favorite quotations to encourage elevated thinking.

The following are from the Text section of *A Course in Miracles*:

- I am responsible for what I see. I choose the feelings I experience, and I decide upon the goal I would achieve. And everything that seems to happen to me I ask for, and receive as I have asked (Foundation for Inner Peace 1992, 448).

- Nothing survives its purpose. If it be conceived to die, then die it must unless it does not take this purpose as its own (616).

- Appearances deceive *because* they are appearances and not reality. Dwell not on them in any form. They but obscure reality, and they bring fear *because* they hide the truth (634).

- Seek not outside yourself. For all your pain comes simply from a futile search for what you want, insisting where it must be found. What if it is not there? Do you prefer that you be right or happy? (617)

- Are thoughts, then, dangerous? To bodies, yes! The thoughts that seem to kill are those that teach the thinker that he *can* be killed. And so he "dies" because of what he learned. He goes from life to death, the final proof he valued the inconstant more than constancy (465).

- From the ego came sin and guilt and death, in opposition to life and innocence, and to the Will of God Himself (417).

- The holiest of all the spots on earth is where an ancient hatred has become a present love (562).

- For as long as you feel guilty you are listening to the voice of the ego, which tells you that you have been treacherous to God and therefore deserve death. You will think that death comes from God and not from the ego because, by confusing yourself with the ego, you believe that you want death. And from what you want God does not save you (233).

- Be not deceived when madness takes a form you think is lovely. What is intent on your destruction is not your friend (493).
- There is no question but one you should ever ask of yourself;—"Do I want to know my Father's Will for me?" He will not hide it (150).
- One thing is sure; God, Who created neither sin nor death, wills not that you be bound by them. The shrouded figures in the funeral procession march not in honor of their Creator, Whose Will it is they live. They are not following His Will; they are opposing it (417).
- The death penalty is the ego's ultimate goal, for it fully believes that you are a criminal, as deserving of death as God knows you are deserving of life (232).
- No one can die unless he chooses death. What seems to be the fear of death is really its attraction (416).
- Death is the result of the thought we call the ego, as surely as life is the result of the Thought of God (417).
- Miracles enable you to heal the sick and raise the dead because you made sickness and death yourself, and can therefore abolish both (4).
- You can rest in peace only because you are awake (158).
- Trials are but lessons that you failed to learn presented once again, so where you made a faulty choice before you now can make a better one, and thus escape all pain that what you chose before has brought to you (666).
- It is still up to you to choose to join with truth or with

illusion. But remember that to choose one is to let the other go (357).

- There is nothing outside you. That is what you must ultimately learn (384).
- When you meet anyone, remember it is a holy encounter. As you see him you will see yourself. As you treat him you will treat yourself. As you think of him you will think of yourself. Never forget this, for in him you will find yourself or lose yourself (142).
- The recognition of God is the recognition of yourself. There is no separation of God and His creation (147).
- The journey to God is merely the reawakening of the knowledge of where you are always, and what you are forever. It is a journey without distance to a goal that has never changed (150).
- You are altogether irreplaceable in the Mind of God. No one else can fill your part in it (179).
- *Now* is the closest approximation of eternity that this world offers. It is in the reality of "now," without past or future, that the beginning of the appreciation of eternity lies (247).

The following are from the Workbook for Students in *A Course in Miracles*:

- Enlightenment is but a recognition, not a change at all (357).
- Deep within you is everything that is perfect, ready to radiate through you and out into the world. It will cure all sorrow and pain and fear and loss because it will heal the mind that thought these things were real, and suffered out of its allegiance to them (63).
- What would you see? The choice is given you. But learn and do not let your mind forget this law of seeing: You will look upon that which you feel within.

If hatred finds a place within your heart, you will perceive a fearful world, held cruelly in death's sharp-pointed, bony fingers. If you feel the Love of God within you, you will look out on a world of mercy and of love (359).

- There is nothing in the world that has the power to make you ill or sad, or weak or frail. But it is you who have the power to dominate all things you see by merely recognizing what you are (361).

- What is a miracle? A miracle is a correction. It does not create, nor really change at all. It merely looks on devastation, and reminds the mind that what it sees is false (473).

- The peace of God is my one goal; the aim of all my living here, the end I seek, my purpose and my function and my life (390).

The following are from the Manual for Teachers in *A Course in Miracles*:

- "Seek but do not find" remains this world's stern decree, and no one who pursues the world's goals can do otherwise (34).

- Remember that no one is where he is by accident, and chance plays no part in God's plan (26).

- What you ask for you receive. But this refers to the prayer of the heart, not to the words you use in praying (53).

- Forgiveness is the necessary condition for finding the peace of God (51).

- Living is joy, but death can only weep. You see in death escape from what you made. But this you do not see; that you made death, and it is but illusion of an end (51–52).

- Joy is the inevitable result of gentleness (13).

- Death is the central dream from which all illusions

stem. Is it not madness to think of life as being born, aging, losing vitality, and dying in the end? It is the one fixed, unchangeable belief of the world that all things in it are born only to die. This is regarded as "the way of nature," not to be raised to question, but to be accepted as the "natural" law of life. All this is taken as the Will of God. And no one asks if a benign Creator could will this (66).

- Teacher of God, your one assignment could be stated thus: Accept no compromise in which death plays a part (67).
- And what is the end of death? Nothing but this; the realization that the Son of God is guiltless now and forever. Nothing but this. But do not let yourself forget it is not less than this (67).

And the following are taken from sources other than *A Course in Miracles*:

- One comes to be of just such stuff as that on which the mind is set. – The Upanishads
- Trust yourself. You know more than you think you do. – Benjamin Spock
- Truth half learned still tends to stay within the range of human reason, mixing good and evil, justifying its false god, the god who was not God enough to create perfect children. – Ruby Nelson
- What is now proved was once only imagined. – William Blake
- Consciously or unconsciously, every one of us does render some service or other. If we cultivate the habit of doing this service deliberately, our desire for service will steadily grow stronger and will make not only our own happiness, but that of the world at large. – Mahatma Gandhi
- Someday, after mastering the winds, the waves, the

tides and gravity, we shall harness for God the energies of love, and then, for a second time in the history of the world, man will have discovered fire. – Pierre Teilhard de Chardin

- If we could read the secret histories of our enemies, we should find in each person's life sorrow and suffering enough to disarm all hostility. – Henry Wadsworth Longfellow

- Some men see things as they are and ask, "Why?" I dream things that never were and ask, "Why not?" – Robert F. Kennedy, paraphrasing George Bernard Shaw

- When you become clear that the reason you want to live to a hundred or more years is so you can express your full creative potential, *you change your chemistry and physiology*. – Deepak Chopra and David Simon

- There is one thing stronger than all the armies in the world, and that is an idea whose time has come. – Victor Hugo

- Concerning all acts of initiative (and creation), there is one elementary truth the ignorance of which kills countless ideas and splendid plans: that the moment one definitely commits oneself, then providence moves too. A whole stream of events issues from the decision, raising in one's favor all manner of unforeseen incidents, meetings and material assistance, which no man could have dreamt would have come his way. – W. H. Murray

- We all have the spiritual power to raise the dead, but we do not believe we have. Our mind does not *unqualifiedly accept* this. – Ernest Holmes

- After all, what is reality anyway? Nothing but a collective hunch. – Jane Wagner

- One way or another, we all have to find what best fosters the flowering of our humanity in this contemporary life, and dedicate ourselves to that. – Joseph Campbell

- Most people have their greatest success after the age of fifty, because by fifty you've made all your mistakes. – Terry Cole-Whittaker
- Whatever we vividly imagine, ardently desire, sincerely believe, and enthusiastically act upon must inevitably come to pass. – Paul J. Meyer
- The glory of God is a human being fully alive. – Saint Irenaeus of Lyons
- You never knew how beautiful you were, for you never really looked at who and what you are. You want to see what God looks like? Go look in a reflector—you are looking God straight in the face. – Ramtha
- Start by doing what is necessary; then do what is possible; and suddenly you are doing the impossible. – Saint Francis of Assisi
- History is a nightmare from which I am trying to awake. – James Joyce
- It is no more in the inevitable order of nature that human bodies should decay as people's bodies have decayed in the past, than that man should travel only by stagecoach as he did sixty years ago; or that messages could be sent only by letter as they were fifty years ago; or that your portraits could be taken only by the painter's brush as they were half a century ago. – Prentice Mulford, 1889
- Every truth passes through three stages before it is recognized. In the first it is ridiculed, in the second it is opposed, in the third it is regarded as self-evident. – Arthur Schopenhauer
- The most beautiful thing we can experience is the mysterious. It is the source of all true art and all science. He to whom this emotion is a stranger, who can no longer pause to wonder and stand rapt in

awe, is as good as dead: his eyes are closed. – Albert Einstein

- What is not brought to consciousness comes to us as fate. – Carl Jung
- I think of the last fifty years as a prelude to my life. – Yoko Ono, on the eve of her fiftieth birthday
- 120 is the new hundred. – Ed Franco
- Pick an age you like and stick with it. – Snoopy

Chapter 10

Single, Whole, Complete

I HAVE TOO OFTEN heard the caution, "Careful, or you'll wind up alone." With so much of society run by its fear of loneliness, it gives one pause to think about the number of people who have entered relationships or gotten married because of their dread of living alone. What is this insidious and ubiquitous fear really about? Usually it's an offshoot of the fear that we won't be able to satisfy our primal needs (i.e., the need to be loved, wanted, and cared about). Intrinsic to the energy that propels this fear is the vision of someone less than able to lead an active life or less than welcomed by others while pursuing such a life. But once we refuse to accept the traditional definition of aging, we immediately decrease the fear associated with being older and alone. If we wake up vibrant and excited about life, it's not very likely we'll spend the day in solitude unless, of course, we choose to.

We all have feelings about loneliness and being alone, and they are worth exploring. What comes up for you? Do you feel guilty, less than, left out, or as if you're somehow not carrying your weight? I had often felt vulnerable about the prospect of being alone on a Saturday night (international date night, as it's been called). I'd had similar, if more intense, feelings on New Year's Eve. Notwithstanding that I always resented being told when to have a good time, it takes a certain amount of autonomy to feel at ease in being alone.

On a societal level, we have a tendency to see people who are single as somehow incomplete. We've been programmed by our culture—through movies, sitcoms, novels, and love songs—to see ourselves as not quite right if we are not romantically involved with someone. We forget that the essential purpose of a relationship is to help us become better persons, not to make us feel better. As anyone who's ever been in a significant intimate relationship will tell you, it's work. If you are not currently partnered, you have a wonderful opportunity to explore what being alone means to you. Often we discover things we never expected. It is usually a welcome revelation when we first realize that we are complete all on our own. Releasing the need to find one's "other half" is its own kind of liberation.

For the bulk of our ancestors, life was about mating and having babies. As such, they were doing their part to keep the species going. Well, our roles have changed. We have enough people now. No longer cave dwellers needing to protect ourselves from danger, the time is ripe to realize the loftiest destiny of humankind—the manifestation of our immortal- or God-self. The core essence of life has shifted from survival to self-acceptance and self-realization, objectives that, paradoxically, allow us to be more effective in community with one another. We are no longer defined by our reproductive capacity, but rather by our contribution to the greater good of humanity. And the best gauge of our success in that regard is our ability to love and be loved.

Years ago, I saw a woman who had written a book called *The Daddy Clock* on a morning talk show. She was talking about the desperate urge to have children that supposedly hits men between the ages of thirty-seven and forty-one. In support of her theory, the male interviewer talked about the longing he sees in the eyes of his childless male friends as they peer into his life and witness the wonders of fatherhood. Albeit unintentionally, their conversation helped propagate the already existing prejudice against persons without children. What about the wonder of living life fully as an adult among other adults? They were right about one thing: It is generally a happier situation for people when they have children, but only because that's how we've set things up.

When asked to identify the turning point for most men, by way of example, the author cited the case of a man for whom the precipitating event was his father's heart attack. Seeing his mother sitting in a hospital waiting room and the subsequent realization that no one would be waiting for him when *his* turn came was overwhelming. What was not discussed as part of the interview was the absurdity of building a family and a life to ensure someone being there for him in case of illness—his real motivation. Maybe if the man in question released his attachment to the fear of getting sick, he might just avoid such a scenario. It certainly wouldn't hurt his chances for well-being if he chose to believe that he is entitled to a personally fulfilling relationship, one in which the primary intent is to be happy, healthy, and alive.

How many individuals would not take a vacation, walk into a restaurant, go to the theater, see a film, or do any one of a number of pleasurable things alone simply because of the fear of judgment or ridicule? Some years ago, I observed firsthand the driving sentiment behind this kind of thinking. I was walking with a friend in Manhattan on a Saturday night when he spotted someone in a restaurant. "Look at that. Isn't that sad?" he said, referring to a woman eating alone. "Hmmm," I said, not knowing quite how to respond. After I got home that evening I remember thinking, "What was so sad about it? She was hungry, didn't want to cook, and was dining out." I have a feeling that if I had delved deeper in conversation with my friend, it would have become apparent that it was more about his fear of being alone than anything else. Instead of verbalizing his own concerns, he projected pity onto someone else.

One reason we find ourselves desperate for romance is because we have been culturally conditioned to be exactly that. Love is somehow supposed to save us. From the time we are little children, it is part of the dream that is foisted upon us: "You will find someone and be happy." Even today there is an implicit yet strident underlying message that, though different according to gender, is equally limiting. For women it is, "You will find someone to take care of you." For men it is, "You will find someone to dominate and protect." Although there's no denying the magic that happens when we find ourselves falling in love, the root of that magic is often infatuation coupled with the unexpressed desire for a better life. I'm reminded of a friend who, on the topic of quitting junk food, said, "Maybe I shouldn't give it up. Maybe doing so would rob me of too much pleasure." We can think of romance in a similar way. Those of us who are spiritual truth seekers know enough to know that the search for love, especially when it's tinged with desperation, is often about fulfilling ego needs. And maybe we don't want to give that up. Maybe we just enjoy the rush too much. There are obviously worse things that a person could be addicted to than romance. But if we're going to indulge our senses and our fantasies, let's make it a conscious choice to do so.

And while we're on the subject of relationships, do not discount or minimize the wondrous benefits and the intensely spiritual rewards to be reaped by joining forces with an animal companion. Although pets, as they are typically called, are viewed by some unenlightened souls as a sad makeshift alternative to having children, many of us know just how richly rewarding the joys of parenting a cat or dog can be. When it comes to expressing love, unconditional or otherwise, you won't find a purer example this side of heaven than that offered by our four-legged friends. They are dearly loved because they represent the highest and the best that life has to offer. No wonder so many people, myself included, will tell you that among the greatest sorrows they have experienced is the death of a beloved animal. In addition to the personal loss, it's also a loss of one of the most benevolent forms of life itself. Those whose perception is sensitive enough are able to see in their animal companions the potential for just how beautiful life can be—potential in us, but realized in them.

Chapter 11

Celebrating Adulthood

ARE CHILDREN MORE VALUABLE than adults? Given how often we are told that children hold the future in their hands, it's probably fair to say that many people think so. One reason for this popular point of view is because we are convinced of our inevitable demise. Unquestionably, from a societal perspective, children are viewed as more valuable than adults. If we look for the psychological basis for this, we don't have to dig too deep to see that adults, particularly older adults, are viewed as closer to death and, consequently, as having less value. Older adults have fewer time chips to spend, it is reasoned. A child doesn't threaten us with thoughts of our own mortality the way an 80-year-old might. It is this author's contention that whereas children are certainly to be revered as precious, so are we all.

Yet even within the context of the socially sanctioned demand to have and raise children, some discrepancies exist. The message is a conflicting one. On the one hand, we're not fully validated until we have children. Without offspring we are somehow seen as not having contributed, not having done our share, or not having been productive—perhaps literally. On the other hand, once the kids arrive, our personal value diminishes with the same swiftness that the focal point of our own life changes. The implicit message then becomes, "All your time should be spent making sure they turn out better than you did." One result of this kind of thinking is that we wind up using our children as an excuse not to work on ourselves. And then, when the kids leave the house and we're in our fifties, we figure it's too late. Many of us know people who fit this description.

More to the point, this philosophy keeps us from celebrating adulthood. We spend much of our lives getting ready for adulthood but, if you really look at it, very little of our energy is put into enjoying it once it arrives. As we first approach it, we have the pressure and demands of school. Once we graduate, the pressure shifts to choosing the most appropriate career and making sure that we take the best steps to strengthen it. There is also commensurate pressure to find the right life partner, fundamentally for the purpose of making certain that we are not alone. Then we have children and the focus shifts to them. At a certain point, somewhere around the forty-year mark, we turn our attention toward retirement readiness and providing for our "golden" years. And shortly thereafter, we start thinking about estate planning to secure our uncluttered departure and to make life as comfortable as possible for those we leave behind. But wait a minute. What, then, was the reason for our being in the first place?

We seem to think that having children will somehow ensure that all our needs in later life will be met. But kids grow up. They are meant to leave. And what happens to the parents who are left with an empty nest and only each other? Not to mention that there's no guarantee that the person you marry and raise children with will be there when those children are grown. A lifetime of unending love between two people is a nice notion, but to expect or demand it seems almost unreasonable. Becoming parents is also seen by some as a reason to stop trying to meet their own needs, so that they can put their children first. Although responsible parenting is, in my opinion, the single most challenging and rewarding job on the planet, many people nevertheless welcome it, on an unconscious level, as the validation of their retreat from self-discovery. In days gone by, a self-sacrificing parent was seen as noble and beneficent. We now know that children respond more favorably to parents who make time for themselves and demonstrate that their own lives have equal value and merit.

Try this bold experiment: Visualize an ideal lover. Let yourself get a clear picture of this person's robust physical attributes. Imagine them as someone who, in colloquial terms, would be, excuse the expression, "to die for." Now quickly imagine that same person at eighty years old. What happened? Do they look substantially different? Did they lose attractiveness? The degree to which the image changed is the degree to which you still believe in aging and death. Since we created these things together through our lack of faith, let's actively uncreate them now.

Go back to your mental picture of the perfect partner. Ask yourself this person's age. The first number that comes to mind will do. Now envision that number pulsing over his or her head in cool blue neon. Bring your focus in closer, so that you're seeing your imaginary partner from the shoulders up. Now, keeping the focus primarily on their face, let the number start to increase one digit at a time. As it does, see their face either remaining the same or becoming more radiant and alive. So, for example, if you started at thirty, when their age becomes thirty-five, they appear as an even greater expression of self. Let the number slowly increase until you reach one hundred. See if you can maintain a firm vision of this person's attractiveness as you do. Resist the temptation to change some aspect of their physicality at around age fifty.

Doing this exercise accomplishes two things: Seeing your partner as continuing in attractiveness over time helps create the space for it to happen; it also effectively tells your subconscious mind that you do not accept the idea that aging must produce negative results. A simple variation of the preceding exercise can be used to reframe your thinking with regard to your own chronological age and how it could affect your physical appearance. It follows in the paragraph below.

Look into a mirror and say aloud, "I am now [insert your present age] years old." While continuing to look deep into your eyes, slowly increase the number one digit at a time. Keep doing this until you say, "I am now one hundred years old." What does it feel like to look in the mirror and see that you look the same at one hundred as you do today? Do you feel foolish? Do you think it's impossible? Remember, we are just beginning to understand how the mind influences the body, and there now exists reasonable cause for hope that no one in good health today need ever wake up to a reflection that is eerily edging toward death.

Once you become aware of the subtle societal message aimed at older adults that says, essentially, "You don't count, you're not good enough," you'll find examples of it everywhere. Sadly, in the eyes of the world, being a fully functioning adult is mostly about measuring how much time you have left. The less time you have left, the less value your life has. And the less value your life has, the less you should care. But I once had the great privilege of witnessing a modest yet dramatic example of someone embodying the polar opposite of this philosophy.

I was conducting a reading and storytelling group at an assisted-living residential facility. One morning the group was graced by the presence of a 92-year-old man named Bill. In an effort to get him to participate, I asked if he would like to share some part of his life with us. Bill thought for a moment and then said, "My life was devoted to my wife and my business. But both are gone now." He paused in the sadness of his statement and then spoke from the heart. "We weren't blessed with children. My wife died a little over a year ago, and I came to live here about six months ago. I don't know what the future holds, but I know I need to get on with my life."

I need to get on with my life. Now, if you asked the average person on the street their reaction to a 92-year-old who says he needs to get on with his life, it's likely that they'd respond, "No he doesn't. He just needs to get comfortable. Because very soon, depending on his faith tradition, he's going to meet Jesus,

Abraham, Muhammad, Lord Krishna, or the Buddha. Or, if he's an atheist, he'll be dust." But Bill was far from the average person's concept of a 92-year-old.

In light of his wife's passing, Bill's statement might have seemed, on the surface, cold or even a bit callous. But nothing could have been further from the truth. As I later learned, Bill had been happily married for sixty-five years; his life with his wife was robust and full. It wasn't that he loved her any less after her death than before, it's just that he also loved life. And now, what choice did he have but to go forward? The message was as profound as it was poignant and dear. As long as we are alive, there is more to do. As long as we are alive, we are a work in progress. As long as we are alive, we need to get on with our lives.

And by the way, getting on with it didn't mean that he wanted to find the equivalent of an Anna Nicole Smith to fuel a sense of late-life sexual bliss or fantasy. Rather, he wanted to partake in occasional social functions, participate in age-appropriate recreational activities and outings, and to attend weekly religious services. As importantly, he wanted to enjoy the company of others while doing these things. In other words, he wanted a sense of community or, to borrow a phrase from a loved one, "to be among the world of the living."

I remember thinking to myself that this man's approach to life could be the antidote to our obsession with youth and our ignoble embrace of aging-related stereotypes. On the spectrum of acts of passive neglect against older adults, I can think of none more repugnant than a tacit lack of respect, of treating someone as if their time is not valuable simply because they may have less of it. Great spiritual teachers throughout the ages have touted the benefits of "living in the now." Here was a man who was doing just that. Wherever you may be today, Bill, I salute your memory and the way in which you touched my life.

Chapter 12

Working Matters

GETTING A SENSE OF one's calling is essential for peaceful living. Many people would gladly forgo the idea of living forever because they so vehemently hate their jobs. As have so many others, I spent more than my share of years doing work for money, which was exactly that, work for money. Though I appreciated the income it provided, I often experienced a gnawing psychological discomfort because I knew it was not how I wanted to spend my time. It is my belief that we are all intended to do work in accordance with our gifts.

The Italians have a wonderful expression: *Ogni bambino è nato con una pagnotta di pane*, which translates to, "Every child is born with a loaf of bread." In its most common context it is used to comfort a mother who has just learned she is pregnant with her sixth child, worried whether the family can afford it. But I once heard it used in a much more poetic way by actor and humanitarian Marlo Thomas, likening our talents and abilities to our "loaf of bread." That is to say, each of us brings at least one unique gift into this world. So what about *your* gift? At your core there is a burning desire, the seeds of which were planted in your consciousness before your birth, maybe even before your conception. You were born with a purpose. The only way you would ever want to achieve physical immortality is by knowing what that purpose is.

If the world is a school, with each of us alternately teachers to and students of each other, knowing what we came here to contribute can only enhance how we play our roles. Marsha Sinetar wrote a book on finding meaningful work called *Do What You Love, the Money Will Follow.* How often have we done it the other way around, chasing dollars and hoping it would somehow bring job satisfaction? We spend more time thinking about what we want for dinner than making sure our career is congruent with our interests. I know too many lawyers who became lawyers because their fathers wanted them to.

Our culture, which is undeniably youth oriented, puts pressure on us to choose our careers early. I remember, as a junior in high school, being given a form to fill out that asked my intended vocation. I broke into a cold sweat. I was fifteen and didn't have a clue. Feeling the pressure to respond, I wrote "veterinarian or math teacher," and then proceeded to worry whether I had to honor that decision for the rest of my life. Many of us don't know what we want to "do" until we pass the age of forty. It makes perfect sense that our gifts would become more apparent as we mature, as we have had that much more time to develop and nurture them. This is something to be celebrated, not denied or refuted. Someone whose insight and compassion might make them an excellent therapist would not necessarily know that at age twenty, or even thirty. Conversely, someone who became a therapist in their twenties or thirties might later realize that their motivation for doing so came from a place of self-denial. As they heal with that issue, becoming an actor or a chef may suddenly seem appropriate.

It used to be that in order to achieve conventional career success, one needed to have an advanced degree in a particular area of specialization. That's also changing. Today there are numerous examples of persons who have attained prominence in their field without holding a university degree in that discipline. It also used to be that once you were established in a chosen career or profession, you stayed with it for forty years, got the gold watch, retired, played golf, and died. By way of contrast, today some people choose careers that last for three to five years and then move on to something else that entices them. We realize that our interests, needs, and desires are not static.

It was always an unrealistic assumption that we could find something to do at twenty-two that would sustain us for the rest of our lives. And now, with the idea of unlimited life looming before us, it makes even less sense to limit ourselves to something we don't truly love, though certainly we *could* find something about which we feel so passionate that we'd want to do it for fifty years. You will find that your various passions have a common link. As much as anything else, they combine to create a vivid portrait of your soul. The point here is that we are always changing, and it is always for the better—if we see it that way. But if we view life as a race against the clock, then pursuing the desire to start a new career at sixty wouldn't make much sense.

Some people's idea of a heavenly existence is one in which they are not challenged on any level. These same people would, I'm sure, look forward to retirement as a time when they would no longer have to work. It's not that they are lazy or don't want to work. Rather, it's that they never thought they were entitled to do work that fed their soul. And so they can't wait to escape the sentence of having to slave the rest of their days. It is this kind of thinking that has imprisoned us in our own perception. But feeling challenged and experiencing joy are not mutually exclusive events within the sphere of gratifying work.

If I told you, "So-and-so is seventy-five years old," and then asked you to describe his or her work life in one word, the word you would likely use is "retired." My mother was a special education teacher whose focus was children with learning disabilities. She adored teaching. Indeed, as I have often said of her relationship to her work, "It was her passion and her life." She worked for the New York City public school system, which, at least during the time of her employment, had a mandatory retirement policy. She was therefore forced to retire during the year of her seventieth birthday. At that time she was what might have been called a young seventy—healthy, energetic, and full of life. And yet, it was a short three years later that she first showed signs of Alzheimer's disease. Even though there is no clinical research that directly links retirement to Alzheimer's disease in a causative capacity, there's no doubt in my mind that she experienced a phenomenon labeled *psychological mortality* by researchers Paul Baltes and Jacqui Smith, who studied older adults. As described by researchers Daniela Jopp and Christoph Rott, psychological mortality is "characterized by the loss of intentionality, identity, psychological autonomy, sense of control, and dignity." In clinical circles it may be called psychological mortality, but we could just as easily call it death of the spirit. Forcibly take away someone's passion in life and it is anyone's guess as to just how devastating or far-reaching the consequences will be.

Work is among the most vital of channels for human self-expression. Freud is generally credited with having said that life consists, in the grand scheme, of two things only—love and work. Through our work, and that includes volunteer work, we can express the highest and greatest that we have to offer. But if we see our usefulness as having a predetermined end, some finite point after which we are no longer adept at our chosen profession, we inhibit our ability to achieve our personal best.

That is not to deny that there is beauty in surrender—the right *kind* of surrender. During the early days of writing this book, I had an experience that was both revealing and humbling. I became physically ill while working a job that I knew wasn't right for me. I developed severe flu-like symptoms and, in fact, couldn't get out of bed. So I surrendered to it. I stayed in bed and prayed for wellness. I also asked to see the lesson behind the malady. On the second day of the illness, as I lay in bed channel surfing, I came upon famed physician Deepak Chopra. He was talking about finding meaning and purpose in one's life through uncovering hidden passion.

As the shortest route to discover one's calling, he suggested reflecting on the question, "If you had all the time and money in the world, what would you do?" Although the answer for me was multifaceted, a key element involved metaphysics and my passion for physical immortality. It was in surrendering to that truth that I created the space in which it could manifest. Although once I had that realization, I thought my healing would be quite rapid: "Okay God, I've done my part; now you do yours. I learned the lesson. Now can I get well?" Evidently, bartering with God doesn't work because I didn't feel fully well for another three weeks. That forced me to consider what it might have meant on an even deeper level. Perhaps I was being overly staunch in my beliefs about wellness and wasn't allowing room for my humanness. That is, maybe the lesson was humility.

One of the first things I did was to create a new life plan. Each time I'd done it previously, it was with the sense of testing the waters. That's all well and good, but at a certain point you have to swim. I did a complete reassessment of my life. I realized there was no spiritual discipline that I practiced with any regularity. Though I had tried to make my life a walking prayer, I didn't have anything to cling to on a daily basis. My spirit and soul had been bereft for a long time and now my body was also breaking down. "Some immortalist," I thought.

Continuing the process of surrender, I soon found myself pacing my apartment, talking out loud to a God I hoped was listening. "My life as it stands now is so lacking in meaning, it's becoming unbearable. I need direction. Please guide me." No booming or mystical voice responded. But allowing for a sense of guidance, I began to slowly walk a new path. I started speaking publicly, without compensation, on the subject about which I was passionate. Meanwhile, I continued to work on my book, holding to the vision that it was meant to be widely read. I also had to take responsibility for the fact that I was the only one accountable for the state of my work life and related financial affairs.

Take a minute now to think about how you might have held yourself back careerwise. Do you have a vision that you have tucked away in the recesses of your mind because you think it's off-the-wall, or because you don't know how to make it happen? These days, there are all kinds of support groups you can turn to for the purpose of making your dream come true. You could even start your own. Now, there may be many things you feel passionate about, and that's good. Make your own top-ten list, those things you would do workwise if you had all the time and money in the world. A list of ten is good because no matter how much you love doing something, if you were going to grace the earth for five hundred years, you could surely have ten careers during your lifetime. And when making that list, let yourself fantasize. Don't try to be practical, logical, or prudent. That's not how we tap our greatness.

When we have trouble deciding on the kind of work we want to do, it is often because we are giving undue power to external voices, the voices of childhood influences telling us what we were expected to become when we grew up. But as an adult with an evolving consciousness, you need to pay attention to what entices you now. No matter how you are earning your living at present, if it doesn't excite you, know that you can still find what does. Really reflect on Chopra's question, as it can be a very useful tool in uncovering your gifts.

Remember too that, regardless of the kind of work you do, you are in part a teacher. As *A Course in Miracles* tells us, we teach what we most need to learn. And so your work is as much about self-discovery as it is about producing results. Let self-expression be the overarching goal of your career. When you discover your passion and are willing to step into that role, the universe notices, and you are rewarded simply for being yourself. And just as the distinction between work and play becomes less clear, your career becomes the natural means by which you channel your creativity. Coming to understand the grander mission of your life, beyond merely earning a paycheck, will bring untold harmony to your daily experience of living.

Chapter 13

Sex and Spirit

N O OTHER TOPICS FUEL controversy as quickly or easily as sex and sexuality. Maybe it's because so many major life issues are, in some way, tied into them. Think about it: procreation, pleasure, pain, conquest, submission, joy, guilt, acceptance, rejection, safety, danger, custom, convention, performance, recreation, business, and, unfortunately, even violence. No wonder sex and sexuality are rarely included in discussions of things spiritual.

Perhaps one reason we recoil from openly acknowledging the significance of sex in our lives is because of how much pleasure it brings. Where did we get the idea that God doesn't want us to experience pleasure? Indeed, it is during moments of intense bliss—and is any moment more intensely blissful than sexual orgasm?—that we touch the face of God. It is in those holy instants that we step outside the realm of time and space and live truly in the now, which just happens to be God's address. But as long as we see ourselves as somehow undeserving of being one with God we will deny ourselves those moments. How could we not feel guilty getting that close to something we believe we don't deserve?

Think for a moment about the role of pleasure in your life. Which of your senses is most closely linked to your heart? What brings you the most physical pleasure? Is it a slow warm bath? A sensual massage? Is there a fragrance you adore? How about a finely prepared meal? Or a particular cold beverage on a hot summer day? Is there any guilt associated with these things? If the answer is yes, you may want to look at how you respond to pleasure in your life and the ways in which you resist it. If your only resistance is to sexual pleasure, you might ask yourself where that message comes from.

Many of us are leery of our sexual energy, fearing where it may lead us. It is intense, dynamic, and can also be overwhelming. It takes courage to face our sexual energy directly. It helps to recognize that it is closely linked to our creativity and self-expression, though we tend to dissociate ourselves from its inherent spiritual nature. In serving as a conduit through which we can express love for others and ourselves, it is actually a sister energy to spirituality. If you deny your sexuality, you will ultimately deny your own godliness.

A good way to make peace with your sexuality is to touch the feelings behind it. Let yourself feel fully sensual and sexual. Get undressed and massage and pamper yourself. Look at yourself lovingly in the mirror. Accept and appreciate the life force that pulses within you. Ultimately, it's about trust. Can you trust yourself as the source of your creativity? Can you trust yourself to be present in the midst of such creative and transformative energy without becoming overwhelmed? The more we can trust, the more we can be present in that energy. The lines between what is sensuous, sensual, and sexual are continually in flux. When we hear a magnificent piece of music that puts us in a reverie, or gaze at a painting that is particularly beautiful, or stare into the face of our favorite flower, we are having a sensuous experience. But that experience is measured on the same scale that calibrates our sexuality. These sensuous moments can be just as fulfilling and exciting as overtly sexual ones.

We hardly ever talk about the explicit nature of sex. Some would argue that it is something to be experienced and *not* talked about. Without question, there is a lack of conscious awareness in this area. We refer to it as "making love," which is often just another attempt at suppressing an aspect of life that we cannot accept. This is not to deny that it can be an extension or expression of love, but it can also be raw and animalistic, a primitive fulfillment of the most basic of instincts, leaving us tired, spent, and sated. And it can be daunting in terms of the sheer physicality of it: the involvement of all our senses, the aerobic expenditure, and the intensity of the pleasure. It is nonetheless a part of the human experience, albeit one that we have historically denied or imbued with shame inherited from generations past.

We also rarely consider the psychological implications of various sex acts. Penetration, for example, has very significant undertones. If one feels good about their partner, it can be an empowering exchange for both. But if unhealed emotions are at play in the relationship (e.g., if the active partner is acting out a form of aggression), the experience of the receptive partner could be greatly affected. Even the act of undressing can tap a spigot of shame related to exposing our bodies. We hold them up to media-influenced ideals regarding size, shape, and body fat that few of us can meet, and we worry if we will be perceived as attractive.

They say the call on the *Titanic* was, "Women and children first!" This has been the customary cry during public emergencies. I would like to suggest that it also echoes societal projections onto women and children as helpless, notwithstanding that they are often less strong than men on a purely physical level. The idea of valuing women's lives more than the lives of men stems from a now deathist fear linked to the propagation of the species, with women seen first and foremost as childbearers and children as having their whole lives ahead of them. Not to mention the manufactured sense of gallantry that many men believe makes them appear honorable: "I will protect you, you poor little thing." But women are neither more nor less capable than men.

When talking about the roles of the sexes, inclusiveness is the key. However, there is also a current tendency, principally for reasons of sociopolitical correctness, to strip the sexes of their inborn differences. This can be equally perilous. Instead, let's fully acknowledge these differences without letting them narrowly define our perception. Are women, by nature, more nurturing than men? Perhaps. Yet it is crucial that we also embrace their innate leadership and managerial abilities. Are men more stoic than women? Maybe. But we must also recognize their capacity to express feelings and to be kind.

It has generally been deemed right and just for men to go to war for their country. It was their inner dictate to step in and sacrifice their lives when things got rough, since, historically, they ran the world and had created most of its misery in the first place. Most men have internalized this unusual mix of power and shame. Even though only a select group of men (i.e., kings, dictators, or elected or appointed officials) declared the wars, all citizens paid the price for it. When we have a truly equitable distribution of power among men and women, the tide will turn toward true equality between the sexes.

For many people, certainly for most men, saying, "I'm afraid," is tantamount to saying, "I'm a failure." But being honest with ourselves about our vulnerabilities and weaknesses, or perceived weaknesses, actually creates strength. One reason the world is in so much trouble is the degree to which men, almost universally, feel the need to be right and in control. This dominating male power needs to be reconsidered and realigned. It is a natural, forward-moving force of nature, but our misuse of it has yielded brutal consequences. Allowed to run amok, it creates wars and devastation.

What a wonderful gift to humanity if men could start to openly acknowledge their fears. As with most cultural phenomena linked to gender identity, the roots of this one have little to do with the way we live today. At one time, men were the protectors, and fear was a signal to opponents that they were in a vulnerable state. So expressing fear posed a real and genuine danger. But what's the danger now? Social ridicule? The potential for being labeled second rate? Much of the undercurrent of anger and deceit among men could be obliterated if they could befriend one another without the fear of being judged. This is particularly obvious in sports, where there is still considerable homophobia. It's as if men are allowed to engage in spirited competition and have fun in each other's presence as long as they make it expressly clear that there is no tenderness between them or feelings shared among them. Nor can they admit that they are enticed by the maleness of the game. But in the final analysis, *macho* is just an acronym for Much Ado Concerning His Organ.

Of equal importance is understanding and embracing the role of lesbian, gay, bisexual, and transgender (LGBT) persons. In the absence of social bigotry and hatred, the percentage of the population born gay could more easily express that unique part of their being. All of us, gay and nongay, would be well served by honoring the gifts of LGBT persons. Since, in many cases, gays and lesbians do not have typical family and child rearing concerns, their focus can more readily turn to the larger human family, bearing witness to the fact that sacred family ties are not dictated by bloodlines. This, in turn, benefits us all.

Independent of one's sexual orientation, given the ongoing evolution of spiritually conscious men and women, our roles are constantly shifting and changing. If you happen to be in a committed, long-term relationship, you have been granted many gifts, and probably more than a few challenges, as a result. Keep the relationship fresh by expressing what is meaningful, real, and true for you. Our responsibility in a relationship is to clearly communicate our needs. In recent decades, a good deal of emphasis has been placed on the importance of conveying one's sexual needs to one's partner. It is, however, equally important that we openly articulate our emotional needs as well.

Change is a slow process, sometimes painfully slow. But we have made enormous strides over the last forty-plus years in this sociocultural arena. Most well-informed people today agree that women are capable of completing any endeavor with a competence equal to that of any man. Young men who view their wives as equals will, as a matter of course, raise their daughters as such. It is the old patriarchal thought system, now mostly viewed as invalid, that has kept women at a disadvantage for so many years. Historically we polarized our feelings and our perception, saying, "This is masculine," and "That is feminine." In truth, we are always balancing elements of the male and female within. One of the differences in this emerging Aquarian Age is that those lines are blurring. We tend to think of men as possessing determination, strength, and power and women as being compassionate, nurturing, and intuitive. Intuition, often considered a female trait, comes from what could be called our feminine side, our receptive yin energy. But each of us needs to cultivate all of these qualities regardless of what gender we happen to be. The more we allow for our individuality, the more thoroughly the stereotypes will break down. There is definitely a "new male." No longer divorced from the feminine, it includes tenderness and compassion as part of its makeup. Similarly, the "new female" is filled with driving, forceful, and productive energies. In a still male-dominated society, the tendency is to try to define women's roles. When we no longer attempt to do so, we will live in the expanse of balanced yin/yang energy, bringing greater harmony to the planet.

Chapter 14

Idols Away

AS A CULTURE WE seem obsessed with looking to others for justification, verification, and validation. We too often act as if anyone—or perhaps more accurately, anyone *else*—knows better than we do. The same impulse that leads us to worship a God-out-there also propels us to create social and cultural idols. This is most evident in the way we treat entertainment and sports celebrities. Instead of seeing them for who they are, talented people to be respected for their gifts, we worship and adore them. Imagine if, instead, we looked within and focused on our own value and worth. There would no doubt be less need for image-making and trendsetting.

As a cultural phenomenon, we also like to tear down our idols periodically, especially those we see as having become *too* successful. Why? Obviously, it stems from the sense that something is lacking in *us*. But nothing is lacking except the knowledge that nothing is lacking. Life is multidimensional and multifaceted; we cannot be and have everything within the range of possibilities all at one time. When we see someone with a particular talent that we don't possess (e.g., a singer or a ballplayer), we tend to think that they are superior and we envy them. But, actually, they just possess *different* talents. Further complicating the matter is that certain talents go unrecognized whereas others hold a particularly high social premium, and this fuels the mechanism that keeps us surface oriented and superficial.

We need only to look at current trends in advertising and marketing to see that we have let the ego run wild. In an odd way, this is a good thing because we can now see where it has gotten us. We've devised a world of fabricated rules and standards, an unnatural interruption of natural beauty. The power and pull of big business has distorted our vision and skewed our reality. Conformity has become a highly marketable commodity, well beyond the realm of the characteristically human desire to be accepted. We now have false ideals as well as false idols; we are told what is "proper" on so many fronts. We forget that we made the rules and then find ourselves enslaved by them, from something as mundane as not eating salad with a dessert fork to the more weighty, like choosing the "right" college.

Turning to outside sources for validation of internal beliefs will invariably create dissonance and strife. No one knows what's best for you better than you. I'm reminded of an acquaintance who worked in the music business. Asked if he could tell which records would become hits, he said, "I can't tell you which ones will make it, but I can tell you which ones won't." Though we may not have *the* answer, we can still know in our heart that it couldn't possibly be God's will to call its children home by destroying the body. When we're aligned with Spirit we become centered and, as a natural result, feel at peace with our ideas, beliefs, and decisions. This might prompt the question, "What about terrorists and suicide bombers who seem at peace with their decisions?" The litmus test for the benevolence of our actions is whether they cause harm to others or impinge upon another's freedom.

Take a moment to think about something you've strived for imagewise, or perhaps something you're still striving for, or maybe even something you've already attained. Ask yourself if your aspiration has been influenced by advertising or the media. Is it something you want for you, or is it something you feel you need in order to fit in? A generation ago, a popular low-calorie breakfast cereal used the anti-fat slogan, "If you can pinch more than an inch," you're probably overweight—a rather strange standard for either health or fitness. At about that same time, I remember my jaw dropping when I saw the cover of a trendy women's magazine sporting a feature article entitled "How To Be Attractive After 30." Funny to think that the mere title of an article could render so compelling an indictment of a culture so devoted to youth and beauty.

Thankfully, evidence of an evolving social consciousness can be found in a more recent advertising campaign. In 2004, Unilever, the company that manufactures Dove soap, launched its "Campaign for Real Beauty," designed to foster self-esteem in girls and young women, especially around issues of body image. The television ads were the result of a research study commissioned by Unilever. Among those overseeing the study were Nancy Etcoff of Harvard University and Susie Orbach of the London School of Economics. Perhaps the study's most revealing finding was that only two percent of the women surveyed would use the word "beautiful" to describe themselves. The researchers further point out that the word "beauty" has, for all intents and purposes, become synonymous with "physical attractiveness." Although among the study's conclusions, we are told, "Authentic beauty is a concept lodged in women's hearts and minds and seldom articulated in popular culture or affirmed in the mass media. As such, it remains unrealized and unclaimed."

Similar ideological distortions have permeated key industries and professions. Take medicine, for example. Whereas graduating from medical school is a remarkable—and a remarkably grueling—accomplishment, why do we think of doctors as more worthy of respect than other professionals? Maybe because we have imbued them with the godlike power to heal. Our forebears are responsible for creating medicine, medical schools, and the medical professionals they produce, and yet so many of us, whether willingly or unwittingly, now hold ourselves hostage to them. As a case in point, I recall seeing a woman on a television news program talking about the day she discovered she had cancer. "I said to my doctor, 'You have to give me six years; I want to see my youngest child graduate high school.' " How sad that she didn't realize that the only person who could give her six years, or sixty for that matter, was herself.

Growing up, I witnessed firsthand the pride and conceit of doctors. While in my late teens, my mother's brother George, a physician, prescribed ampicillin for her. When I asked him the difference between ampicillin and penicillin, he responded, "I would explain the difference, but it would only confuse you." He could just as easily have said, "Ampicillin is a synthetic derivative of penicillin and covers a broader spectrum of bacteria." My mother had five brothers, each of whom became a doctor. With the exception of one, they were among the singularly most arrogant persons I encountered as a child and young adult. Two were dentists, three were gynecologists. I always thought one of them should have become a proctologist; then they could have opened a practice called No Holes Barred.

Self-acceptance and self-love are the keys to personal transformation. Consider the ways in which perhaps you do not love yourself. Do you consider yourself worthy of being pampered? Would you lavish upon yourself the same level of care and attention that you would give to a lover or dear friend? Do you realize the scope of your own brilliance? Somehow, in getting bumped and bruised along the road of life, we often answer no to these questions.

I once had the experience of working for a woman who weighed at least three hundred pounds. When I first met her, I found her appearance somewhat off-putting and found myself making all sorts of silent judgments—I figured she came with a lot of emotional baggage. But she turned out to be warm, genuine, and kind. I was so touched by who she was that it even once brought tears to my eyes. Yet in the eyes of the world she might have been routinely disparaged for being significantly overweight. But that was only her external form; the beauty of her soul and spirit was clear. Blessed with a sharp wit, she was quick to make light of her life without being self-denigrating. In a culture as judgmental as ours, her size was a ready invitation to become self-loathing. But she chose not to buy into that. I'm not saying that, from a health perspective, she wouldn't have benefited from losing weight. My point is that she didn't look to other people for validation.

Our magnificence is something we have somehow forgotten. Or maybe we've been told to forget it. If you took an inventory of your personal self-worth, you might feel differently. I strongly recommend that you take the time to make a list of the things you've achieved in your life on spiritual, social, and intellectual levels that reflect the uniqueness of you.

Complete the following sentence: "Some of the things that make me unique are … " These do not have to be big things. In fact, they can be quite the opposite. Look for aspects of your personality that could too easily be overlooked in the world we inhabit. If you are someone who customarily extends kindness to strangers (e.g., complimenting a new mother on the beauty of her baby, holding a door for someone merely as a courtesy, offering your seat to a fellow passenger simply because he or she looks tired), write it down. If you are someone who learns from your mistakes and tends not to repeat them, write it down. If you are a spouse, parent, or guardian and have a love in your heart that guides, drives, and motivates you, write it down. If you selflessly offer guidance or support to another on a regular basis, write it down. If you have overcome an obstacle, physical or emotional, of which others may be largely unaware but of which you are particularly proud, write it down. My hope is that you will come to realize that you have many unique and wonderful gifts that might not have been acknowledged or recognized by others.

Let's stop the habit of putting public figures on pedestals. I had hoped that the one good thing to come out of the O. J. Simpson/Nicole Brown tragedy, aside from pointing out the need for increased education on domestic violence, would have been our coming to view celebrities in a more realistic light. I think we still often assume that if fame has touched a person's life, an innate goodness somehow goes along with it. But talent and greatness are not necessarily coexistent attributes. There are many people who are immensely talented but hardly great. Conversely, there are some people who lack exceptional talent but are clearly great. Mother Teresa comes to mind. Her greatness was in the degree to which she cared. But how many people get booked on *The Tonight Show* for caring?

Chapter 15

Choosing to Choose

WHEN FIRST HEARING ABOUT the concept of physical immortality, people tend to point a finger and say, "Wow, there's someone living in denial." But a true immortalist willingly looks at all aspects of life and death and comes to his or her beliefs through sober contemplation. Do you, in this moment, feel even a glimmer of the possibility that there could exist a God that does not want to kill you?

What do you believe is the reason you are alive? What is the purpose of your life? What does your God look like? How will you age? Is aging necessary? Is death inevitable? Are you going to die? Sadly, most of these questions usually get answered for us before we even get to ask them.

The world's problems are not your problems, as much as some people would like to convince you otherwise. The only life you are responsible for is your own. We are all here to learn and evolve; moreover, we are all co-creators of the world around us. So blame has no role here. Unfortunately, the word "blame" and the word "responsible" are often used interchangeably in our culture. Think of a mother with three prepubescent children who, upon discovering that an heirloom vase has been broken, gathers them together and asks, "Who is responsible for this?" But in the way in which I'm using it, "responsible" is a word of empowerment. There is liberation in taking responsibility for our lives. We are responsible because we are powerful and our actions have definite consequences. Like it or not, we have created every part of our collective and individual unhappiness. Collectively, we have brought forth impoverished nations, famines, and wars. Individually, we have wrought bankruptcy, anorexia, and hate crimes. We all draw to ourselves the experiences we need for our own evolution although, granted, while living through them, it may not feel that way. Any challenge or obstacle, no matter how limiting it appears, involves choice. At the very least, we can choose how we feel about it. Choice is the greatest gift we've been given, as precious as life itself, for it is our choices that alter our circumstances and, consequently, our destiny.

That which we call truth is as much a choice as anything else in life. Choosing immortality calls for far more than merely claiming it; it requires understanding the truths behind it and the willingness to do the work to achieve it. And willingness is the key. Are you willing to see your life as a series of opportunities to help you realize your full potential? Are you willing to look at your life honestly and openly? Are you willing to release your negative programming? If you could take a metaphorical sponge and magically cleanse your brain of all limiting ideas, would you erase the thought that death is inevitable? Many would opt in favor of death because, simply put, life is too much work. But in doing the work, some amazing things happen. Our lives start to flow, our life urges increase, and we start wishing it were possible to beat death.

It's not easy to acknowledge that we bear responsibility for the unpleasant aspects of our lives. It's a lot easier to look outside ourselves and place the blame there. I once again recall my stint at that organization in which there was little structure or leadership. We continually passed the buck or, more accurately, the blame. It was a classic case of, "It's not my job." But in the end, every judgment against someone else is an attempt to avoid looking at what we don't like in ourselves.

With self-scrutiny, however, comes the risk of self-judgment. Consider the example of a former cigarette smoker who develops lung cancer. For that person to judge himself or herself would in no way support the intended result, health and healing. Increasing one's own guilt or fear is an almost certain way to negate the effects of a life-affirming immortalist philosophy. We must remember that we control our thoughts. If something unfortunate happens and, as a result, someone throws guilt our way, we do not have to join them in their assessment. We can instead say to ourselves, "Yes, I'm responsible for my health, and yes, I have a cold right now, but no, I do not blame myself. I accept this as part of my personal process." The irony is that in letting go of the blame, we heal more quickly.

In order for you to seek immortality in earnest, your life will need to closely parallel your idea of paradise. You are entitled to be peaceful, centered, creative, prosperous, spiritually fulfilled, and to have loving relationships, abundant energy, and radiant good health.

What is it that would keep you from wanting to live forever? Do you get up every morning and go to a work setting that you detest because you think there is no alternative? We are limited only by our imagination. If money is keeping you tied to your job, realize that your employer is but one source for your financial supply. When our mind is receptive to it, money can come from a multitude of sources. Whatever your present life circumstances, others have had similar or worse challenges and found ways to make them work to their advantage. Because they didn't give up. Because they believed. Yes, faith moves mountains. But we first must believe that it is within our power to move them.

Those of us who espouse physical immortality as a lifestyle are not antideath per se. There are situations in which one may feel complete with their time on earth and be ready to move on to do work in the spirit realm or to reincarnate under new life circumstances for a completely different learning experience. But it should be a conscious choice. Those who choose to die have as much choice in the way they die as in the way they live. Death can be a peaceful transition; there does not have to be a major accident or illness. There is no reason that a life lived peacefully should end any other way.

Some people have a hidden wish to die because their life isn't working and, whether consciously or unconsciously, they think of death as a cure-all for their problems. "I'm already fifty years old, so why should I change? Why bother to start a health and fitness program for the first time in my life? It's more than half over, so I may as well just ride it out." Although giving voice to thoughts like these is not socially condoned, our unconscious can think them quite easily. Only by coming to believe that time is on our side can we do the things we feel called to do. If you are stuck in the belief that you must die because you see it as part of the so-called natural plan, then consider the giant sequoia tree that lives to be over two thousand years old. If you can't yet imagine humans escaping the birth/death cycle, then at least consider that plant life might have done so. Anything that allows the flicker of immortality into your conscious awareness will work to tremendous advantage in terms of your own process.

I remember how much I dreaded birthdays, with thoughts like, "Oh God, another year closer to death. Will the signs of aging start now? Will I soon get the aches and pains I'm told are sure to come?" Conversely, I can vividly recall a morning early in my process of integrating a belief in physical immortality. I awoke with the most incredible feeling, fully joyful at the prospect that if it were not a certainty that I would die, then everything, in time, could be worked out. In other words, there was joy in allowing for a God that didn't want to kill me. But as long as we think we must die, a part of our mind will remain fearful. And nothing kills joy as quickly as fear.

In these times of uncertain economies, shifting political and geographical landscapes, and tensions of an amazing variety, we may duly wonder why a world was created in which humankind seems opposed not only by nature but by humankind itself. A conscious acknowledgement of our role as co-creator with Spirit would accelerate positive large-scale change. We still hear talk about the cruelty of a God that could allow children to die during wars or famines. Yet man continues to create wars. And even though there is enough food on the planet to ensure that no one goes hungry, we let children continue to starve.

Every moment of our existence is fraught with choice, a choice between ignorance and understanding. Our decisions will foster confusion or clarity, illusion or truth; they cannot coexist. Eventually the choice comes down to death or life. We can think of the gift of immortality as lying behind a locked door at the end of a hidden passageway that few have entered. Thankfully, the key is in our hand, and the lock is on our side of the door. Most of us have witnessed the consequences of berating ourselves as not good enough, as needing to mend, repair, or restructure our lives before they could be considered acceptable. We can, instead, choose self-acceptance. Accepting ourselves exactly as we are honors the life force in, through, and around us. And that, in turn, is reflected in our bodies. A self-affirming choice is, ultimately, a rejuvenating one.

Chapter 16

Living in Paradox

To become truly immortalist is to live, at least for the time being, in the land of the fantastic. The rational mind would never—could never—comprehend immortality because, at the risk of stating the obvious, immortality is beyond the scope of its comprehension. Spirit, on the other hand, is mercurial, ephemeral, and mysterious. We cannot predict it. Though most people feel that they *can* predict, with virtual certainty, the maximum number of years they will live. Spirituality is also laden with paradox. For instance, the road to God-consciousness is a cooperative effort, traveled with support from and interaction with fellow humans encountered along the way. And yet, our revelations, insights, and healing—indeed, our very lives—unfold individually. We realize our destiny, great or small, alone. It turns out that the movie of your life is a private screening for two—you and God.

Consider also the way in which we view and use time. Most of us have had the experience of being able to share a laugh over what once caused us heartache. It's interesting to consider what actually changed in those situations with the passage of time. Only our perception. It therefore stands to reason that if we could learn to change our perception independent of time and see the bigger picture more often, we might experience more joy in our lives.

In our lack of understanding of how spiritual laws work, and given our propensity to use illusory physical evidence to negate the wholeness of our being, we have mistakenly concluded that life must end in death. By all appearances, it seems to be an undeniable fact that people age, get sick, and die; the proof, as it's called, is everywhere. But using that "proof" to negate our innate potential is, pardon the pun, a grave mistake. The reason life has ended in death for just about everyone is because just about everyone has believed that it must. If form follows thought, then having the thought that death is inevitable lurking in our unconscious will surely, in time, kill us.

Let's not forget that we are also highly praised if we prepare for our own demise early in our adult lives. This shows responsibility, it is argued. Those who make arrangements for their own tidy exit and disposal are held in high regard. If we put half as much energy into the art of living as we put into worrying about how we might be judged by those who survive us after we're gone, we would double our life span in no time.

Another reason death is so frequently accepted without protest is because of the hardship we encounter on a day-to-day basis. But much of that would disappear if we fully embraced our station as creators or, at the very least, co-creators of the world we see before us. We would also feel an increased sense of freedom and ease relative to our worldly duties, for our primary concern would be extending kindness to our brothers and sisters. Many who strongly clutch the belief that aging and death are inescapable have themselves an unconscious desire to die. And can you blame them? If all you were ever told from the time you were a child is that one day you will grow old and die, why get excited about being here?

Heaven lies in the present moment. *Now* is the most meaningful time any of us can live in, through, or for, because all of eternity exists within it. Whenever we project into the future, we deny our potential for bliss, which can only be experienced in the here and now. That is not to say that planning isn't a consequential aspect of life. To be sure, it is. But the focus should always be the present. For example, when planning a future event, the joy lies in the act of planning. I know, I know, I can hear you already: "What about root canals?" As with most things in life, what we resist persists. Pull against the knot and the knot grows tighter. Though it's nearly a given that some highly unpleasant, albeit necessary, physical experiences will remain part and parcel of life on this planet, no earthly good can be achieved by approaching them with fear or dread. Some of the women may be thinking, "This guy's never given birth." But I have endured physical pain in a variety of situations and circumstances and, in each case, when I was willing to *be* with the pain, it never failed to lessen its grip, at least to some degree.

There are those who say we can learn to take pleasure from virtually any experience if we are fully present while it is happening. I haven't reached the point in my personal evolution where I can say that this is true for me. I once dislocated my shoulder and the nearest hospital was over an hour away by car. During those sixty-plus minutes, in which I writhed in excruciating pain, if someone had offered to shoot me to stop the agony, I'd have quickly responded, "Oh yes, *please*, pull the trigger." Nonetheless, I believe it is possible to transcend pain.

Of course, physical immortality also begs the question of overpopulation. During the sixties, there was much speculation that the world would soon be overpopulated and there wouldn't be enough food come the turn of the century. Now that we've reached the third millennium, the idea has arisen that there may not be enough people to populate the workforce needed to provide adequate services to the world. But the universe never thinks in terms of numbers; it knows that life will find a way. Surely many people will continue to leave the planet, either as a conscious choice or a soul choice. What's more, anyone attaining spiritually-based physical immortality would likely realize that we are all interrelated and that bloodlines have little to do with what constitutes a family. They would consequently be more conscious about the decision to have children, relative to what that means on a global scale.

Annalee Skarin, in her book *Beyond Mortal Boundaries*, suggests that we have preagreed to our purpose in life before coming to the planet. Some come to learn lessons and then contentedly return to their life on a non-physical plane. A popular T-shirt of some years ago that read, "Just Visiting This Planet," comes to mind here. Others incarnate for different purposes, such as to teach by their example. We should respect everyone's path. There are those for whom the idea of living forever may be repulsive and for whom, based on their soul's path, it may be a bad idea. But if you feel called to consider it as a possibility for yourself, honor that. You may be on the planet for entirely different reasons than your friends or any member of your family.

It would seem that, in a world as in need of love and compassion as ours, those whose desire to stay is predicated on service to humanity would be allowed to do so. Still, some see the wish for physical immortality as a mask that hides the fear of death, others as the grandiose imaginings of the ego. Ironically, the more we allow for the existence of death as appropriate and valid in the lives of those who remain allegiant to it, the more we are able to free ourselves from its bondage.

If you buy an exercise video, somewhere early in the presentation, ostensibly for the purpose of protecting you from potential harm, you will see a standard legal disclaimer: "Before beginning this or any other exercise program, it is a good idea to consult with your doctor." Well, exercising my First Amendment right, I'd like to say that a consultation with a doctor, particularly one chosen without great care, could also be a source of potential harm. They, more than other caring professionals, seem wedded to the idea of aging, sickness, and death. Although there are some remarkable minds now practicing medicine, as a whole, physicians still tend to be a predominantly deathist group. Now, as I mentioned earlier, when I dislocated my shoulder, I went to a doctor, just as I would call a plumber if I had a major drain problem. But would I then ask the plumber why my lights are flickering? Well, ditto for doctors when it comes to longevity. I still remember the sickening jolt that I felt during a conversation with a 91-year-old woman who was dealing with depression. Not uncommon for persons in that age cohort to seek professional help from their primary physician first, she had approached her internist with her concerns. His response? "Of course you're depressed, you're ninety-one." Just because someone is in a highly esteemed position, it is no guarantee that they have your best interests in mind. Anyone who believes, implicitly or explicitly, that you must age, get sick, and die is not really supporting you.

Very shortly after my introduction to immortalist philosophy, I attended a lecture by psychiatrist Gerald Epstein, author of the book *Healing Into Immortality*. At the time, I didn't know that he championed the idea of physical immortality. As he was speaking (I believe the subject of his talk was healing imageries), I soon realized that some of the things he was saying sounded immortalist in nature. So I raised my hand and questioned him. "Are you saying that we can live forever?" "Yes," he responded, "I believe it is possible." Not ready or willing to accept the concept at the time, I countered, "Do you think it could be your ego that has you believing you can live forever?" Completely undisturbed by my challenge, he casually replied, "I do think it's possible to live forever, but if I don't, that's okay too." It is that kind of tranquil resoluteness that opens the door to the infinite and the miraculous.

We must demonstrate patience with others and ourselves as we evolve into this new paradigm. Let's remember that life, as we currently know it, is a dense form and that manifestation takes time. Recognizing the true source of our being allows us to be present in the world, to give and receive as we deem appropriate, but always with the willingness to let go. As an immortalist, I do not advocate holding on to life just for the sake of holding on. I do suggest holding on if one is interested in making the world a better place. A common response when one is first introduced to the idea of physical immortality is, "Who'd want to be stuck here forever?" The reason we think in terms of being stuck here is because we have not yet fully developed spiritually. But if our earth becomes the paradise it was intended to be, who would want to leave it?

Chapter 17

Let It Shine

As we begin to functionally live the truth that God is everywhere and in all things, we will come to understand that this includes us. The human body is as awe-inspiring as the cosmos. In many ways the body is a veritable microcosm, as all the wonders without are also within. The cosmos has an indefinite life span and so shall we, once we have integrated this truth. As we move along the spectrum toward immortality, we will gain a greater reverence for human life, indeed, for all life. As the global compassion quotient rises, we will see a proportionate rise in the frequency with which people reach out to one another as instruments of healing. And isn't that our ultimate purpose—to support and nurture other humans on their way to their full realization of self?

Once we have fully removed the veils to our understanding of the workings of Spirit and higher consciousness, we will know a love so bright, beautiful, and pure that all the years of contemplation, dedication, and preparation will surely have been worth it. It is at that point that we will claim our immortality.

But we cannot do it alone.

Those of us who feel called to spread the word that death is not inevitable should step forward now. As more and more of us do, the concept will become less and less outrageous. Eventually, people might just as casually ask someone, "Are you an immortalist?" as they would ask, "Are you a vegetarian?"

Remembering that your thoughts and words are living, vibrant things, use them to your advantage to create your experience of life. Most of us have someone else's idea of heaven planted securely within us. But it is *your* idea that holds the key to the mystery of your existence. There will come a time when we will recognize that anything that promotes death or dying is not—could not be—of God. G-o-d could just as easily be spelled L-i-f-e. Reject all limiting beliefs, refuse to judge by appearances, renew yourself in the stillness, attune yourself to your divine purpose, and you can't help but become enthusiastic about life.

Sometimes we just need to hear someone say, "It's possible," before we can make something real. One reason that death has had such a stranglehold on humanity is because very few people have been willing to stand up and say, "It can be defeated." Well, count my voice among the growing number of those who say it can. Death can be defeated. And you can live as long as you'd like. But here's the rub: The only person who can give you the gift of immortality is you. All any book, ideology, or discipline can do is spark your desire, but you make it happen. It takes commitment, the courage to take an unflinching look at the beliefs you hold, and the personal resolve to release those that are not in your best interests. From this point onward, each time a decision is before you, ask yourself if your choice will take you backward or forward, negate or support you, favor death or life. Even seemingly small decisions usually do one or the other.

Imagine a world in which rushing was reserved for actual emergencies, in which we appreciated the little things, and in which we dedicated every day to the richness of Spirit rather than to the call of the ego. Whatever your vision, the time has come to actively manifest it. At least give it your sincerest attention, as that which we focus on gathers energy. Many people are now taking the time to form organizations with alternative visions for the future of our planet, hoping that the collective minds of those involved will bring about the realization of their vision. It takes only mental energy to start the fire. Once lit, it will spread from mind to mind and a new world order will appear in form.

My personal vision includes a world characterized by unconditional positive regard for every individual under all circumstances. Imagine two patients in a hospital, one a sanitation worker, the other a physician. Now imagine that the attending medical personnel treat both of them with the same level of care, attention, and respect. That scenario may be as close a depiction of an earthly paradise as any I could envision, that is, a world in which we are always mindful of providing nurturing support to our brothers and sisters without considering the outer circumstances of their lives. I realize it sounds idealistic and unrealistic. Yet I firmly believe it is our ultimate destiny as humans.

This world was intended as the holy temple of the good and the beautiful, but we have not allowed it to unfold. Instead, our fears have kept us shrouded in darkness. We have propagated a belief in evil, but evil doesn't exist. What appears as evil is ignorance ignited by fear. And the only way to supplant this destructive flame is by allowing the light of our spiritual magnificence to shine in its stead. Are you willing to release violence, famine, sickness, and poverty from your mental imagery? Disengaging these thought patterns from your own consciousness will help eradicate them from the world. Whatever it is that would keep you from wanting to live forever, you can release it. You are worthy of perfect health. You deserve a body that serves you, one that is filled with energy, strength, and light. You are entitled to joy.

We all intuitively know something is missing from life on this planet as we've known it thus far. That something is unconditional kindness extended between and among all people. As we begin to revere human life as truly sacred, the childlike qualities of innocence, faith, trust, and hope will be naturally rekindled in each of us. Those traits reignited—active, passionate, and burning in the hearts of all living persons—will allow us to experience the joys of heaven here on earth.

And so, this book concludes with a question that I asked early on. What is *your* vision of paradise? Whatever it is, it comes from a holy place. You didn't think it up yourself; God put it there, and it is the key to creating an eternal future.

Left unexplored, the specter of death will consume us. We can, however, choose instead to shine light upon its darkness and embody a truth as yet still hidden somewhere beyond our imagination. Immortality is worth pursuing. It's worth the effort. It's worth the time. It's *not* worth dying for.

References

Baltes, Paul B., and Jacqui Smith. "New Frontiers in the Future of Aging: From Successful Aging of the Young Old to the Dilemmas of the Fourth Age." *Gerontology* 49, no. 2 (2003): 123–135.

Chopra, Deepak. *Quantum Healing: Exploring the Frontiers of Mind/Body Medicine*. New York: Bantam Books, 1989.

Dyer, Wayne. *There's a Spiritual Solution to Every Problem*. New York: HarperCollins, 2001.

Epstein, Gerald. *Healing Into Immortality: A New Spiritual Medicine of Healing Stories and Imagery*. New York: Bantam Books, 1994.

Etcoff, Nancy, Susie Orbach, Jennifer Scott, and Heidi D'Agostino. "The Real Truth About Beauty: A Global Report." Report, Unilever, 2004. Accessed November 21, 2009. http://www.campaignforrealbeauty.com/uploadedfiles/dove_white_paper_final.pdf.

Foundation for Inner Peace. *A Course in Miracles*. 2nd ed. Mill Valley, CA: Foundation for Inner Peace, 1992.

Gass, Robert, and On Wings of Song. *Om Namaha Shivaya: Tenth Anniversary Deluxe Edition*. Spring Hill Music SHM 6018.2, 1996, compact disc. Originally released in 1986.

Groger, Lisa, and Jessie Leek. "Images of Ohio Centenarians: An Exploratory Study." Report, Scripps Gerontology Center, Miami University, 2008. Accessed November 21, 2009. http://www.scripps.muohio.edu/research/publications/documents/Cent_report.pdf.

Hay, Louise L. *You Can Heal Your Life*. Carlsbad, CA: Hay House, 1987.

Holy Bible, New Living Translation. Wheaton, IL: Tyndale House Publishers, 1996.

Jopp, Daniela, and Christoph Rott. "Adaptation in Very Old Age: Exploring the Role of Resources, Beliefs, and Attitudes for Centenarians' Happiness." *Psychology and Aging* 21, no. 2 (2006): 266–280.

Keyes, Ken, Jr. *The Hundredth Monkey*. Coos Bay, OR: Vision Books, 1984.

Leadbeater, C. W. *The Chakras*. Wheaton, IL: Quest Books, 1927.

Markey, Judy. *The Daddy Clock*. New York: Bantam Books, 1998.

Nelson, Ruby. *The Door of Everything*. Camarillo, CA: DeVorss, 1963.

Ray, Sondra. *Celebration of Breath*. Berkeley, CA: Celestial Arts, 1986.

———. *Lasting Love Relationships*. Sound Horizons ISBN 1-879323-23-0, 1993. Audiocassette.

Ray, Sondra, and Bob Mandel. *Birth and Relationships: How Your Birth Affects Your Relationships.* Berkeley, CA: Celestial Arts, 1987.

Rivers, Joan, with Richard Meryman. *Enter Talking.* New York: Delacorte Press, 1986.

Siegel, Bernie S. *Love, Medicine & Miracles.* New York: Harper & Row, 1986.

Sinetar, Marsha. *Do What You Love, the Money Will Follow.* New York: Dell, 1987.

Skarin, Annalee. *Beyond Mortal Boundaries.* Camarillo, CA: DeVorss, 1969.

Standing Room Only: Lily Tomlin in Appearing Nitely. Television program. New York: HBO, August 14, 1979.

Weil, Andrew. *Spontaneous Healing: How to Discover and Enhance Your Body's Natural Ability to Maintain and Heal Itself.* New York: Ballantine Books, 1995.

Williamson, Marianne. *A Return to Love: Reflections on the Principles of "A Course in Miracles."* New York: HarperCollins, 1993.

World Food Programme. "Hunger." World Food Programme. Accessed November 21, 2009. http://www.wfp.org/hunger/faqs.

Suggested Reading

Byrne, Rhonda. *The Secret*. New York: Atria Books, 2006.

Capra, Fritjof. *The Tao of Physics: An Exploration of the Parallels Between Modern Physics and Eastern Mysticism*. 4th ed. Boston: Shambhala Publications, 1999.

Chopra, Deepak. *Ageless Body, Timeless Mind: The Quantum Alternative to Growing Old*. New York: Harmony Books, 1993.

————. *Quantum Healing: Exploring the Frontiers of Mind/Body Medicine*. New York: Bantam Books, 1989.

Chopra, Deepak, and David Simon. *Grow Younger, Live Longer: 10 Steps to Reverse Aging*. New York: Harmony Books, 2001.

Cohen, Gene D. *The Creative Age: Awakening Human Potential in the Second Half of Life*. New York: HarperCollins, 2000.

Epstein, Gerald. *Healing Into Immortality: A New Spiritual Medicine of Healing Stories and Imagery*. New York: Bantam Books, 1994.

Foundation for Inner Peace. *A Course in Miracles*. 2nd ed. Mill Valley, CA: Foundation for Inner Peace, 1992.

Gawain, Shakti. *Creative Visualization: Use the Power of Your Imagination to Create What You Want in Your Life.* Novato, CA: New World Library, 2002.

Gupta, Sanjay. *Chasing Life: New Discoveries in the Search for Immortality to Help You Age Less Today.* New York: Warner Wellness, 2007.

Hay, Louise L. *You Can Heal Your Life.* Carlsbad, CA: Hay House, 1987.

Holmes, Ernest. *The Science of Mind.* New York: Tarcher Putnam, 1966.

Jampolsky, Gerald G. *Teach Only Love: The Twelve Principles of Attitudinal Healing.* Hillsboro, OR: Beyond Words Publishing, 2000.

Kurzweil, Ray, and Terry Grossman. *Fantastic Voyage: Live Long Enough to Live Forever.* New York: Penguin Group, 2004.

Leadbeater, C. W. *The Chakras.* Wheaton, IL: Quest Books, 1927.

LeBlanc, Donna. *The Passion Principle: Discover Your Personal Passion Signature and the Secrets to Deeper Relationships in Love, Life and Work.* Deerfield Beach, FL: Health Communications, 2006.

Mulford, Prentice. *Thoughts Are Things.* Radford, VA: Wilder Publications, 2007.

Nelson, Ruby. *The Door of Everything.* Camarillo, CA: DeVorss, 1963.

Ponder, Catherine. *The Healing Secrets of the Ages.* Camarillo, CA: DeVorss, 1967.

Ray, Sondra. *Celebration of Breath.* Berkeley, CA: Celestial Arts, 1986.

———. *Drinking the Divine.* Berkeley, CA: Celestial Arts, 1984.

———. *Essays on Creating Sacred Relationships.* Berkeley, CA: Celestial Arts, 1996.

———. *Healing and Holiness.* Berkeley, CA: Celestial Arts, 2002.

———. *How to Be Chic, Fabulous and Live Forever.* Berkeley, CA: Celestial Arts, 1990.

———. *Inner Communion.* Berkeley, CA: Celestial Arts, 1990.

———. *Interludes with the Gods.* Berkeley, CA: Celestial Arts, 1992.

———. *Pure Joy.* Berkeley, CA: Celestial Arts, 1988.

Ray, Sondra, and Bob Mandel. *Birth and Relationships: How Your Birth Affects Your Relationships.* Berkeley, CA: Celestial Arts, 1987.

Roizen, Michael F., and Mehmet C. Oz. *YOU: Staying Young: The Owner's Manual for Extending Your Warranty.* New York: Free Press, 2007.

Sher, Barbara. *I Could Do Anything If I Only Knew What It Was: How to Discover What You Really Want and How to Get It.* New York: Dell, 1994.

Siegel, Bernie S. *Love, Medicine & Miracles.* New York: Harper & Row, 1986.

———. *Peace, Love & Healing.* New York: Harper & Row, 1989.

Sinetar, Marsha. *Do What You Love, the Money Will Follow.* New York: Dell, 1987.

Skarin, Annalee. *Beyond Mortal Boundaries.* Camarillo, CA: DeVorss, 1969.

Steinem, Gloria. *Revolution from Within: A Book of Self-Esteem.* Boston: Little, Brown and Company, 1993.

Tuttle, Esther Leeming. *No Rocking Chair for Me: Memoirs of a Vibrant Woman Still Seeking Adventure in Her 90s.* Bloomington, IN: iUniverse, 2003.

Walsch, Neale Donald. *Conversations with God: An Uncommon Dialogue, Book 1.* New York: G. P. Putnam's Sons, 1995.

Weil, Andrew. *Spontaneous Healing: How to Discover and Enhance Your Body's Natural Ability to Maintain and Heal Itself.* New York: Ballantine Books, 1995.

Williamson, Marianne. *A Return to Love: Reflections on the Principles of "A Course in Miracles."* New York: HarperCollins, 1993.

Yogananda, Paramahansa. *Autobiography of a Yogi.* Los Angeles: Self-Realization Fellowship, 1993.

About the Author

Edward Franco, MS, is a therapist who specializes in treating older adults. He worked for more than a decade in social services as a vocational counselor with disadvantaged populations. He is a student of *A Course in Miracles* and a lecturer and group facilitator. As the creator of Regent Hospital's "Humor and Healing" workshop, Ed was featured in *The New Yorker*'s "Talk of the Town" column. He lives in Manhattan.